Understanding the Divide

Understanding the Divide

A Presbyterian Elder, a Roman Catholic Theologian,
and Basic Questions of Christian Faith

Lyle K. Weiss S.T.D.
and
Thomas M. Tasselmyer

RESOURCE *Publications* · Eugene, Oregon

UNDERSTANDING THE DIVIDE
A Presbyterian Elder, a Roman Catholic Theologian, and Basic Questions of Christian Faith

Copyright © 2018 Lyle K. Weiss and Thomas M. Tasselmyer. All rights reserved. Except for brief quotations in critical publications or reviews, no part of this book may be reproduced in any manner without prior written permission from the publisher. Write: Permissions, Wipf and Stock Publishers, 199 W. 8th Ave., Suite 3, Eugene, OR 97401.

Resource Publications
An Imprint of Wipf and Stock Publishers
199 W. 8th Ave., Suite 3
Eugene, OR 97401

www.wipfandstock.com

PAPERBACK ISBN: 978-1-5326-3718-6
HARDCOVER ISBN: 978-1-5326-3720-9
EBOOK ISBN: 978-1-5326-3719-3

Manufactured in the U.S.A.

All scripture quotations in the contributions of Lyle K. Weiss are taken from the New Revised Standard Version Bible, copyright 1989, Division of Christian Education of the National Council of the Churches of Christ in the United States of America. Used by permission. All rights reserved.

All scripture quotations in the contributions of Thomas Michael Tasselmyer are taken from the Holy Bible, New International Version®, NIV®. Copyright © 1973, 1978, 1984 by Biblica, Inc.™ Used by permission of Zondervan. All rights reserved worldwide.

To my beautiful wife Terry and my wonderful son Noah, sacraments of God's presence and grace, who daily fill my life with joy, hope, and love. They are the two most powerful embodiments of the transformative love of God in my life and to them I dedicate this book.
Lyle K. Weiss
on the occasion of our son Noah's birthday, January 31st, 2018

To my wife Laurie,
whose pure and simple faith in Jesus inspires me.

Tom Tasselmyer
February 1, 2018

Contents

Introduction
    Thomas M. Tasselmyer | 3
    Lyle K. Weiss | 10

Part I—Scripture: What Role Does the Bible Play in Your Church?
1. God's Word in Human Words | 17
2. Our Ultimate Authority | 27

Part II—Salvation: What Does Your Church Teach is Necessary to Attain Heaven?
3. Salvation by Faith Alone | 41
4. Heaven: The Fulfillment of a Relationship | 56

Part III—Sacraments: What are the Sacraments in Your Church and What Do They Do?
5. Sacraments and the Continuing Mission of Jesus Christ | 73
6. God's Grace Made Visible | 101

Part IV—Saints: What Does Your Church Teach About the Faithful Departed?
7. Sainthood: The Vocation of All Who Believe | 123
8. Saints: Models of Discipleship | 134

Part V—Structure: How Does Your Church Organize and Operate Local Congregations?
9. Of Institutions and Kingdoms | 151
10. Presbyterianism: Representative Church Government | 165

Contents

Conclusion
    Thomas M. Tasselmyer | 185
    Lyle K. Weiss | 193

Bibliography | 201

Introduction

Thomas M. Tasselmyer

One of the best things about being an elder in my church is the opportunity the position affords me to meet with people who are considering formal membership. I especially enjoy it when I meet someone with a Roman Catholic background who is not quite sure what the differences are between Reformed Presbyterianism and Roman Catholicism. I feel like I have a special connection with these brothers and sisters in Christ because that's who I was too.

My first memories of life in the church go back to my early teens after our family had moved from my hometown of Baltimore, Maryland to Fairfax, Virginia, and I was serving as an altar boy at St. Leo's Catholic church. I'm pretty sure that all of us who served as altar boys were there because our mothers wanted us to serve and probably had visions of us becoming priests or, maybe even, the first American-born pope! But for me, pleasing my mother was a bonus because, I actually enjoyed being an altar boy.

I liked belonging to the team. We were led by a drill Sergeant-like leader, Father Diamond, who instilled in us the importance of doing the job right. Father Diamond insisted on punctuality, clean cassocks and surplices, proper posture, and hands held with palms against each other, fingers pointing up toward heaven, thumbs overlapping in the shape of a cross. I remember learning to delicately pour wine from gigantic jugs into tiny crystal containers before each service, the smell of incense, lighting the altar candles, pouring water on the hands of the priest as he prepared for communion, the weight of the over-sized bible we held for the priest to read the Gospel, worrying that my arms would tremble if the reading for the day was too long, and the honor of being chosen to serve in weddings and funerals.

I was frequently assigned to serve at the 6:30 a.m. weekday mass which meant rising before dawn to grab a bite to eat before mom drove me to the church. We entered a sanctuary that was dark, except for a few lights over the altar. The pews in the huge space were nearly empty; typically, only me, the priest, my mom, and maybe another parishioner or two were there. It was very quiet, no music or singing, the priest barely audible as he whispered the mass. Those early mornings serving as an altar boy in the cool darkness, alone with my thoughts, the candles, and the familiar prayers of the mass, all made a deep impression on me.

And there are other fond memories of life in the Catholic church too. They include staying up late for midnight mass on Christmas Eve, ashes on the forehead at the beginning of Lent, the palm branches on Palm Sunday, kneeling before the crucifix on Good Friday, holy water, and the purple, white, red, and green colors of the clerical vestments and altar cloths that changed according to the church calendar.

When I reflect on these memories I realize they were all ways in which the church formed my awareness of holy times, holy places, and holy things, all of them created and ordered by a very holy God. I knew God and felt His closeness with all of my senses. For me, growing up in the Catholic tradition was about learning how to love and deeply respect—or, as the Bible says, fear—a holy God. The Psalms are filled with the blessings that flow from such an experience: "The Lord confides in those who fear him,"[1] "Blessed are all who fear the Lord, who walk in obedience to him,"[2] "the Lord delights in those who fear him, who put their hope in his unfailing love."[3]

Fast forward thirty years from my altar boy days and I was worshiping with my wife, Laurie, and our four sons, in a Presbyterian church where I became an elder. I do not believe anything happens by accident. Read the Bible, study theology, or just look back over your life and you will discover what theologians call God's providence. Everything happens according to God's eternal plan, and He providentially carries out His plan by governing everything and everyone in His creation. For me, the decades-long journey from Catholic altar boy to Presbyterian elder is a winding one with a story of divine providence too complex to recount here. But looking back, I can see God's handiwork.

God's plan was for me to attend North Carolina State University, not only to study meteorology, but also to meet Laurie, a beautiful girl from

---

1. Psalm 25:14.
2. Psalm 128:1.
3. Psalm 147:11. All Scripture is quoted from the New International Version (NIV) translation of the Bible unless otherwise noted.

Introduction

Raleigh with a sweet southern accent, and a heart for Jesus. We fell in love and started to think about marriage but, I was a Catholic, and she was a Protestant, and both of us were struggling to understand the divide.

So, she gave me a book to read; *Clap Your Hands!* by Larry Tomczak. I found the book helpful because I could relate to Tomczak's experience growing up in the Catholic church, and, most importantly, his discovery that Christianity is more than religious obedience opened my eyes too. I began to realize that I needed to know and trust Christ on a personal level. That realization helped me, and Laurie, understand the divide between her Protestant experience and my Catholic upbringing, a crucial last step before she would say "yes" to my marriage proposal. Laurie and I have now been married for thirty-three years and understanding the differences between our faith backgrounds has strengthened our love, drawn us closer together, and, I believe, made each of us better disciples.

God's perfect plan also included Hunt Valley Church. That's where Frank Boswell's theologically rich sermons, and one particularly intriguing Sunday School class that introduced me to the systematic theology of the Westminster Confession of Faith, triggered in me a need to know God with my mind, to explore the rational side of my faith. Seemingly overnight I wanted to understand God theologically. The more theology I read and studied, the more my studies felt like worship; I felt closer to God and I needed to dig deeper. I was discovering what the apostle Paul meant when he encouraged the church in Rome to "be transformed by the renewing of your mind."[4]

An insatiable desire to know more about what I believed, and why I believed it, led me to want to pursue a master's degree in theology. But since I work the night shift, evening classes didn't seem possible, except at one school. St. Mary's Ecumenical Institute is just a couple of miles from the television station where I work, and they offered a master's degree program with classes perfectly timed during my dinner break. So, I enrolled, and for four and a half years I hurried over to the campus between newscasts to enjoy an hour of studying theology in classes taught by wonderful professors like Lyle Weiss, and to marvel at the beauty of the rational precision of my faith. God is holy and yes, He is knowable.

I was also thoroughly enjoying God's ironic way of orchestrating His plans. It was surely not an accident that I was studying theology on the campus of America's oldest Catholic seminary, alongside priests, pastors,

---

4. Romans 12:2.

and laypersons from virtually every Christian tradition, and being taught by Protestant, Orthodox, and Catholic professors. And it was a treat when I could arrive early for class and visit the beautiful chapel. It was almost always empty and nearly dark, only a dim light or two shining over the altar, just like those early mornings at St. Leo's. Sitting there in that quiet and holy place, praying before my class began, I felt as if I had come full circle. In my youth I had discovered the holiness of God as an altar boy in the Catholic church. Now, as a Presbyterian, I was discovering God again, in theological studies on the campus of a Catholic seminary. It was all an affirmation, in my mind, that God does not see us as Catholic or Presbyterian, He loves us all and "rewards those who earnestly seek him."[5]

Growing up in the Catholic church shaped me spiritually in a way that compliments the spiritual growth I have experienced in a Reformed church. In the early days of my walk with Christ I was steeped in Catholic traditions and I learned to know and love God with my heart. In more recent years I have discovered the beauty of the Reformed faith and its emphasis on knowing and loving God with the mind, and immersing yourself in His revealed Word. Jesus told us to "Love the Lord your God, with all of your heart, soul, mind, and strength,"[6] and I can now see how my bifurcated faith journey has helped me do that.

In my experience, the Catholic tradition excels at spiritual disciplines, it highlights the mysteries of our faith, and it emphasizes the holiness of God. The Reformed tradition excels at organizing our faith in a comprehensible systematic theology. It is not opposed to mystery, but it seeks assurance, and so most who worship in the Reformed tradition become, to some degree, theologians. They study the Word of God to explain and strengthen their faith. They practice what St. Anselm called, "faith seeking understanding." And that is what most attracted me to the Reformed tradition.

In the passage from Mark's Gospel that I cited before, when Jesus told the Jewish scholar how to love God, He quoted what is known as the *Shema*, from the Hebrew for "hear," the first word of the passage every faithful Jew knows: "Hear, O Israel: The Lord our God, the Lord is one. Love the Lord your God with all your heart and with all your soul and with all your strength."[7] The *Shema* lists three dimensions of loving God: heart, soul, and strength. But Jesus added one more: the mind. That is not

---

5. Hebrews 11:6.
6. Mark 12:30.
7. Deut. 6:4-5.

surprising; Jesus, after all, was a teacher. He spent three years instructing His closest followers and then told them to go and make more disciples, "teaching them" what they had learned.[8] Using the mind that God gave us in a quest to learn more about Him is part of how we love Him.

So, the greatest commandment is to love God with all our heart, that is, from the very core of our being and with all sincerity; and with all our soul, meaning with passion, emotion, and affection; and with all our strength, which is enthusiastically and zealously; and with all our mind, not with a blind devotion, but with the fullest understanding possible of who it is we love. I hope this book will help you understand that both the Reformed and Catholic traditions offer different ways to love God the way Jesus wants us to love Him, and tapping into the best of what each side has to offer may help you love God that way.

In the pages that follow I will try to explain how Reformed theologians understand the doctrines of: Scripture, salvation, sacraments, saints, and the church's structure. Reformed theology is the understanding of God and His purposes that grew out of the sixteenth century Protestant Reformation. It emphasizes the sovereignty of God, the authority of Scripture, and salvation that only comes through faith in Christ by the grace of God. In addressing the topics in this book through the lens of Reformed theology I will rely heavily on my understanding of the Westminster Confession of Faith.

The Westminster Confession of Faith is the product of Puritan clergy and theologians who met at Westminster Abbey in London, England, from 1643 to 1648. They were tasked by Parliament to further reform Anglicanism. Using earlier confessions of faith, the historic creeds, the preaching and writings of other Reformed scholars, and, of course, Scripture, they produced a summary of Reformed Christian doctrine that is still viewed by many Reformed theologians as comprehensive, clear, practical, and faithful to the Word of God.

The Westminster Confession of Faith was brought to America by immigrants from Scotland and Northern Ireland and became the confession used by various Presbyterian churches in America. In the Presbyterian church where I am an elder, we look to the Westminster Confession of Faith, and the Westminster Larger and Shorter catechisms, as the standards of our theology.

---

8. Mathew 28:20.

In Part One I hope to show why the Bible is so important in Reformed theology. I will touch on what the Bible is, how Reformed theologians interpret it, and why we think it is our only infallible source of special revelation from God; the only source of truth that can bind the conscience of a Christian.

In Part Two my goal is to explain why Reformed theologians take a monergistic view of salvation. I'll explore why, in the Reformed tradition, we believe our salvation is completely dependent on God, and how our only hope to withstand His judgement is for God, Himself, to come and rescue us.

Part Three is where my job becomes a lot less strenuous than Lyle's. In the Reformed tradition we have only two sacraments, compared to the seven that Lyle has to explore! So, I'll try to explain the discrepancy in the number of sacraments, and what Reformed theologians believe the sacraments are, how they work, and what they do.

In Part Four I again have it easier than Lyle because the Reformed tradition has a less extensive doctrine of saints than our Catholic friends. But, I'll look at what the Bible has to say about who the saints are and how we should think about them. In this chapter I'll also explore ideas regarding the Reformed understanding of what happens when we die.

Part Five will address the way a church is organized in the Reformed tradition, especially the Presbyterian form of church governance. In this chapter I will also try to give some insight as to why the aesthetics of a Presbyterian church are so much different than most Catholic churches, and why our worship services are structured with the sermon as the focus instead of the Eucharist.

Finally, in a brief conclusion, I'll share some ideas on how I believe Catholics and Protestants should seek unity in their diversity.

If you take your faith seriously, if you are a devoted Catholic, or steadfastly Protestant, and believe that what your tradition teaches is true, it can be very stressful to even talk about your faith with someone from another tradition. Some of the people who come to our church from a Catholic background share with me their sense of guilt for leaving the tradition they grew up in. Given the "us against them" attitude that can still be found within Christianity, that is understandable. I recently saw an advertisement trying to convince Catholics who had "left" the church to "come home," with the clear implication that worshiping in another denomination was equivalent to running away from Christ. I really wish the advertisement had said, "Come worship Christ with us, or wherever the gospel is preached!" The original Westminster Confession of Faith, written in the seventeenth century, called the pope the Antichrist; sadly, some in my tradition may still believe that. Referring to each other as runaways or heretics does not in any way strengthen the body of Christ. The goal of this book is not to convince you to run away and attend my church, or go home to Lyle's church. The goal is to convince you that we should try to understand the divide between Catholics and Protestants so that we can enjoy each other's rich traditions, share each other's strengths, and support each other's unique ways of taking the gospel into the world.

Lyle K. Weiss

THIS BOOK WAS BORN out of friendship. It was a friendship that developed over a period of years with Tom while I was serving as Professor of Systematic and Moral Theology at St. Mary's Seminary and University's Ecumenical Institute and Tom was pursuing his Master's Degree in Theology. Tom had taken several courses with me during his theological pursuit. The coursework soon spilled out into hallway conversations after class or, after I left St. Mary's, an occasional dinner. In addition to discussions about our families and careers, the conversation always ventured into theology and the current state of the church generally and parish and academic ministry specifically. Our similar experience in both parish and academia and our commitment to the theological mission of the church was evident in each of those discussions. What Tom and I quickly realized was that many of his adult parishioners and my undergraduate, and some graduate, students often possessed a very rudimentary understanding of their own faith tradition. The questions we often encountered affirmed this sensibility. While we sat around a dinner table sharing high minded philosophical and theological concepts, our parishioners were interested in learning more about the basic foundations of our distinct Christian traditions.

As a result, Tom and I decided it might be a good idea to provide our parishioners with a book that would reflect on some of those basic questions and the foundational knowledge they were seeking. That decision provides this book with its basic framework. The five chapters explore basic theological foundations of our faith traditions. The chapters focus on the topics of scripture, salvation, sacraments, saints, and structure. (It would be more accurate to say church structure but that would ruin the alliteration.) The chapter divisions flow from the questions we have been receiving over the past decades in our work both in parish communities and in the academic community. We understand the chapters do not, nor are they intended to,

INTRODUCTION

provide an exhaustive introduction to all facets of the theological systems of these two faith communities. But, we believe they represent a sound and helpful first step in the process of discovery and the effort to grow deeper in knowledge about what we believe. Faith tells us that we believe. Theology reflects meaningfully on what we believe. This book sets for itself the task of reflecting meaningfully on what we believe as Presbyterians and Roman Catholics about basic questions of Christian faith.

Each year, theological volumes are published which are written by experts largely for experts, which is why in our culture, many of these volumes sadly do not receive a broader reading. This book does not set out to be included in that robust and worthwhile list. I used to joke with my graduate students that the great Jesuit theologian Karl Rahner would write a fifty-page article in which the first 45 pages were spent clarifying what he was not going to be addressing and the final five pages were spent complaining that time would not permit him to treat his subject in more depth. Though an exaggeration, I offer it as a reminder that books by experts, as valuable and necessary as they are, often do not address the concerns of ordinary believers in language that is easily accessible and intelligible. This volume will no doubt contain much that might make experts wince and it may at times lack the clarity experts would want to offer. I want to state up front, I wholeheartedly agree. As with any book, the author looks at the finished version and sees far more opportunities to improve the manuscript than glory in its successes. For any failings in the book, for times when I should have chosen different emphases, and for any missed opportunities to better introduce the faith of the Roman Catholic Church as I understand and continue to wrestle with it, I take full responsibility. Our hope, however, is that this book will provide an adequate door through which many can enter into the depth and breadth of our broad and profound Christian theological tradition. The dean of American Civil War historians, James McPherson, has commented (though he is not alone), that nowadays scholars know more and more about less and less. To use a medical analogy, scholars are specialists and not general practitioners. For example, my area of theological specialization concerns the moral significance of the bodily resurrection of Jesus. This book, however, does not possess such single-minded focus. Rather, it functions as a handbook from a general practitioner. It is my hope that what is offered in a general way will be sufficient to invite readers to reflect upon these basic questions and hopefully generate sufficient interest and desire to pursue greater knowledge of their own tradition and the traditions of other communities.

I should also point out that, though I am a Roman Catholic theologian, I am not writing as an official representative of the Roman Catholic Church nor am I offering the official answers articulated by my community's leadership. There are vehicles already available for those who simply want the 'official teaching' (See the Catechism of the Catholic Church). Even reflection on basic questions leads us to consider issues about which there exists a wide range of scholarly opinion. When discussing foundational subjects, it is important to thoughtfully consider such questions, knowing that the answers we encounter can lead us down very divergent paths. Even varying emphases can greatly affect our destination and the path pursued to reach it. I, therefore, do not write as an official representative of the Roman Catholic Church but as a theologian and believer in conversation with fellow believers wrestling with these basic questions of the Christian faith, talking through the meaning of scripture, salvation, or the saints, pondering together the many questions these important subjects raise. The thoughts I offer in the chapters that follow clearly originate in the Roman Catholic tradition to which I belong and in which I was shaped and formed both personally and professionally. But, in the interest of full disclosure, the reader should know my reflections are not intended to state the official position of the Roman Catholic Church on these issues. For clarity, I try to indicate where and when I am deviating or meaningfully reflecting on alternative positions. Nevertheless, I am proud to be a Roman Catholic theologian and I am fully aware that the substance of my contribution to this volume flows from my study and consideration of my tradition and the traditions of other communities of faith through the years. I have tried to curtail any impulse to sound academic in my writing and strive to address in intelligible and widely accessible language basic questions that are of interest to believers. I want to apologize in advance if and when I violate my commitment to that effort. In addition, I want to point out that stylistically, we have tried throughout this volume to avoid long columns of footnotes that are distracting to many readers. We want the book to read, not like an academic tome, but, as mentioned earlier, as a conversation between fellow believers in an honest pursuit of truth.

We live in a world in which a person's interpretation of his or her religious tradition has significant consequences. Having witnessed terrorists fly airplanes into buildings, run into crowded marketplaces with bombs

Introduction

strapped to their chests, or learned of radicals who shoot abortion doctors or blow up abortion clinics, the world has become keenly aware of the power of religious interpretation. But, the importance of religious interpretation is not limited to those who would use religion as an excuse for violence. For example, the bible is used to justify any number of moral stands taken by citizens across the United States, informing the views of many when they head to the ballot box on election day. The so-called 'culture wars' often involve a religious sensibility, at least for some involved in the clash of worldviews. It was an element of the introductory lecture of my Introduction to Scripture course I gave to my undergraduate students that we live in a world shaped in many ways, for good and ill, by religion and the bible. To possess some level of understanding of both is not only our religious duty but it is also our duty as citizens of the nation and the world.

To understand what we believe, what we do, and why is a necessary dimension of meaningful participation in the life of our faith community. Many Roman Catholics each Sunday perform numerous actions, the origin and meaning of which are mostly unknown to them. Hands are dipped in fonts of holy water, people genuflect to a tabernacle, and bow before an altar. These are behaviors that, for many believers, are informed more by memory and training than by understanding. Jesus exhorts us to "Seek first the kingdom of heaven,"[1] but for many of us, no matter how sincere our desire might be, the kingdom is not sought first but perhaps fifth, after financial, technological, political, and cultural literacy. Or, sixth perhaps if we include sports knowledge and seventh if we include binge watching our favorite shows. Many of us possess a genuine desire to grow in knowledge of our faith but lack the hours in the day. Between our time at work, our time commuting to and from work, helping our kids with their homework, preparing meals, keeping the house one step ahead of complete chaos, and doing our best to stay aware of the news, little time is left for study of our faith's theological tradition. Tom and I used to commiserate about offering adult formation opportunities to our communities that would often be poorly attended. Years ago, back when I was a seminarian, it was very frustrating. As a husband and father, it has become far more understandable. Therefore, I invite you to think of this book as an adult formation session with the ability to pursue these important topics at your own pace, respectful of the many demands you confront, and without the need to leave the comfort of your own home.

1. Matt. 6:33.

Understanding the Divide

This book began in friendship and has been supported throughout the writing process by friendship. It is my hope that sharing reflections on what we believe and why will make a small contribution to promoting the friendship that should exist between our two communities. We live in a world, and are citizens of a nation, intensely divided on a wide variety of issues and concerns. Too often, that division affects families, nations, political parties, and faith communities. Like those on opposite sides of the political divide, too often faith communities share a suspicion of the other because of the stereotypes and false notions we may have accepted about each other through the years. It is true that we may not agree with each other on every point of faith. Some of those disagreements might be insignificant while others might be tremendously so. But, at the end of the day, we are all Christians called to faith and discipleship by the same Lord, Jesus Christ. To deepen our knowledge and love of him through thoughtful reflection on the beliefs of our two communities and to strive to bring together more closely in the bonds of faith and hope those who call upon his name is the larger purpose of this book.

Part I

Scripture

What Role Does the Bible Play in Your Church?

Chapter 1

God's Word in Human Words
Lyle K. Weiss

What is the Bible?

THE BIBLE IS A collection of books with designs on us. To enter into the study of the bible is not like studying the military strategy of the Duke of Wellington when confronting Napoleon at Waterloo. One can pursue such study and have the contours and substance of your life remain largely unchanged. The voices of those who have walked the stage of history desire that they only be remembered and perhaps understood. But, the biblical authors want to change your life. They seek not to highlight the economic, political, social, or military history of their times, though such realities are often very important for understanding the author's message. Rather, they seek to share news they hope will reach into your heart, transforming your thoughts, your feelings, your values, and your life. It is of course possible to read and study the bible without being moved or transformed by it. But, such transformation is the intention of the authors and the God who inspired them to write the good news for the benefit of later generations. This collection of books wants to say something to us about who God is and who we are created and called to be in light of God's presence and love.

The bible is the foundational document for two of the great world religious traditions, Christianity and Judaism.[1] As such, it contains the foundational narratives that give birth to these two great traditions and

---

1. The biblical figures of the bible are important also to Islam, though the Qur'an is their central holy book.

Part I: Scripture

establishes the core values and beliefs that guide the life and development of these religions through the centuries. The bible contains the written expression of their experience of God in history. To understand either of these two communities requires some sense of these foundational stories. Certainly, it is necessary, if one wants to understand what it means to be an American, to have some sense of the foundational stories of the nation. We cannot understand what it means to be American without some basic understanding of the Revolutionary Period and certainly the Civil War. So too, it is not possible to understand what it means to be a Jew or a Christian without some basic grounding in the stories and the people whose experience of and response to God brought these two faith communities to birth. In that sense, the bible is a normative or foundational document. One cannot understand or enter into the Jewish faith without some awareness of the TaNaK,[2] the Jewish scriptures, any more than one can enter into Islam without some awareness of the Qur'an. That is why Americans continue to debate the proper interpretation of the two founding documents of the nation, the Declaration of Independence and the Constitution. They are normative documents that articulate the basic sense of who we are as a people and as a nation so understanding them appropriately is a necessary and ongoing conversation. So too, one cannot enter meaningfully into the Christian faith without some basic encounter with the stories of ancient Israel, Jesus of Nazareth, and the early church. To say the bible is normative is to suggest that it is foundational and will always be deeply and necessarily involved in the self-definition of the people and communities born and shaped by it.

The questions raised by this section's topic swirl around the issues of the authority of the bible, biblical inerrancy, biblical infallibility, inspiration, and interpretation of the bible. These are vital components of the larger search for the truth. The pursuit of the truth is indeed a complex quest within the framework of the Roman Catholic Church. Though it is certainly true that the bible occupies a central location in that quest, the existence of the bible has certainly not made the search any easier. Interpretations of the bible can reveal very diverse approaches and understandings of the bible as a whole and with regard to the interpretation of particular passages within it. We know as Americans, for over two centuries, the United States has been guided by the Constitution. However, the mere existence of that

---

2. TaNaK is an acronym for the the Hebrew Scriptures, broken down into three sections: the Torah (the law), the Nevi'im (prophets), and the Kethuvim (writings).

foundational document has not eliminated tensions and disagreements. In fact, the proper understanding of the Constitution is itself a highly debated topic involving the work of highly trained scholars and legal professionals along with interested and active citizens. Like the Constitution in American life, the bible occupies a privileged place in the Christian church's pursuit of truth. But, the Catholic quest involves not just the bible but the continuing inspiration of the Holy Spirit, the work of theologians through the centuries, the statements of popes and bishops, the very definition and understanding of tradition, and the witness of the faith and wisdom of the living, believing community. Defining and understanding the key and complementary roles played by such diverse actors is critical to establishing the place and role of the bible in the Roman Catholic tradition.

Catholic thought often distinguishes between capital and lowercase realities. There is sacrament with a lowercase 's' which refers to those people, places, events, etc. that reflect the presence of God. Then there are the uppercase 'S' sacraments, the seven special vehicles of grace of which we shall say more later. From the Roman Catholic perspective, truth is built on the one source of Tradition (capital T), consisting of sacred scripture and the tradition (lowercase 't') or teaching of the church, both of which flow up from the same wellspring of God's self-revelation. Protestant believers shaped by the battle cry of the reformers "Sola Scriptura," may wonder why scripture and tradition are set on equal footing in the Catholic tradition. The reason this is so is because, in the Roman Catholic view, to put it one way, the bible does not produce the people of God but the people of God produces the bible. The gospels, for example, are written by believers for already established believing communities. Paul is a believer and a pastor writing to communities that he or others have already established. Each of the writings of the New Testament is produced by believers proclaiming the good news, and the ramifications of that news, for the benefit mostly of those who already believe and are members of believing communities. Many of Paul's letters in particular are written by a pastor to communities experiencing difficulties in their living of the faith they had received. To state it another way, the church has already been in existence when the writings of the New Testament are produced. The community has already been baptizing, celebrating the Eucharist, and proclaiming the good news well before the New Testament authors put quill pen to parchment. The New Testament writings, though occupying a privileged place in the tradition of the church, are nevertheless part of that tradition and not existing above, beyond, or distinct from it.

In addition, the Catholic community does not believe the Holy Spirit stopped speaking at the close of the canonical period, that period during which the books that would eventually be officially regarded as the church's canon were written. Encountering the word of God is a complex process involving the original authors, the Holy Spirit, and the believing community in every age. Contemporary biblical scholarship has articulated the distinctions between the text, the world behind the text, and the world in front of the text. Truth is never simply a matter of the printed word but of the encounter between that word and the living community shaped by and proclaiming it. For the Catholic Church, the truth has an evolutionary character to it, our ability to appreciate and grasp it and live in light of it is not simply assent to ancient writings but the ongoing encounter between the word and the church as it exists in each successive generation.

Such a view recognizes that the biblical literature itself is a complicated collection of writings involving some truths that are bound to the time and place in which they were written and some that are possessed of truths that are timeless, not bound by the conventions of geographical location or historical context. In each generation, the faith and wisdom of the believing community, open always to the movement of the Holy Spirit, must determine which truths the bible articulates possess timeless significance and which represent the time-bound expressions of truth that attach to specific communities at a particular time in a distant past but no longer have infallible relevance for the contemporary community of faith. This is simply to recognize there might be a difference between the believing community's affirmation of the New Testament claim that Jesus is Lord and its rejection of the perennial need to follow certain dietary regulations, choose acceptable cloth for clothing, or how to respond to the children of our enemies in battle.

In the Catholic tradition, the bishops are the official interpreters of the bible, aided and substantially abetted by legions of biblical scholars and theologians through the centuries. As you might imagine, as is no doubt true for debates within a wide variety of Christian traditions, the official interpretation of the bishops rarely, if ever, definitively settles the matter of biblical understanding. In truth, in most circumstances such an official interpretive body does not and should not override the individual believer's ability to encounter the biblical literature in a meaningful and spiritually beneficial way. Many believers can read a passage in the comfort of their own home and recognize the spiritual import for their lives without recourse to any official interpretation of the church or the use of a biblical commentary written by scholars. The official interpretation of the bishops often applies to those situations in which the believing community is dealing with a difficult passage or its application to a contemporary issue of faith and morals or some aspect of the theological tradition like the identity of Christ or the structure and governance of the church. Catholic believers can, and are encouraged, to incorporate bible reading into their daily prayer lives, integrating sacred scripture into the daily expression of their relationship with God through Jesus in the Spirit.

But, the Catholic tradition is more than simply an expounding on the meaning of scripture in each new age. To return to our analogy of the American experience, the Revolutionary and Civil War periods are critical to understanding American identity and mission. But, the Constitution required the work, developing thought, and fresh insights of later generations of Americans to resolve the issue of slavery intentionally left undone at the convention in Philadelphia as we would need the work, commitment, and transformation wrought by the thousands of citizens in the Civil Rights Movement who stood for the recognition of the full equality, freedom, and dignity of all citizens a century later. The bible is a normative but not solitary source of truth flowing from the wellspring of the Holy Spirit. Rather, the bible is one foundational source of grace among other sources, most notably the Sacraments (capital 'S'). If it is true that the Reformed tradition focuses primarily on the pulpit, the Catholic tradition focuses simultaneously on the altar and the pulpit. Though a later chapter will take up the topic of sacraments more intentionally, it is necessary to note at this juncture that the Sacraments are vehicles of grace equal in stature to the biblical narrative. According to the council fathers of the Second Vatican Council (1962-1965), the Eucharist is the source and summit of Christian life.[3] The council fathers affirm "the Eucharist is the sum and summary of our faith."[4] It is the Eucharist that nourishes the Christian spirit and strengthens the community of believers for the challenge of responding faithfully to the call of Christ to follow him for it is in and through the Eucharist that the believer receives the very body and blood of Christ, accepting it into his or her very person. The ancient Christian principle lex orandi lex credendi (the law of prayer is

---

3. Flannery, *Vatican Council II: Volume 1*, Lumen Gentium, 11,
4. Ibid.

Part I: Scripture

the law of faith)[5] stresses the centrality of the church's liturgical tradition. This ancient axiom states that before there was a common creed or an agreed upon biblical canon, there was the liturgy of the church. It was the church's prayer that provided the theological framework for establishing the creed and the canon. Therefore, in the Catholic tradition, the liturgy is a unique source of truth. Yet, that is not to diminish the power of the word, for the Catholic mass involves and includes both sources of grace, wisdom, and inspiration for Christian living. However, it is to suggest that for Roman Catholicism, we are not a tradition of the bible alone.

Authority of the Bible

The authority of the bible is a complex reality for the Catholic Church. While acknowledging the sacred scriptures as the divinely inspired word of God, it recognizes nevertheless that its human authors used their own gifts and abilities in the process of writing down what God inspired them to communicate. According to the teaching of the church, the biblical books contain what God wished his people to know for the sake of their salvation. But, the church often retreats from using the word inerrant when speaking of the biblical literature. To speak of papal infallibility, the church limits the pope to defining infallible teachings when speaking ex cathedra (from the chair) on matters of faith and morals. Though there are many teachings that are given the presumption of truth, infallible teachings must be identified as such and offered in communion with the bishops of the church. There have been precious few claims of infallibility though many dimensions of the church's teaching authority fall under the principle of American jurisprudence, innocent until proven guilty. In that sense, the bible is infallible when articulating the knowledge human beings need to know for their salvation. Inerrancy, however, is the belief that the bible is without errors because it flows from the mind of God and is the communication of his word to humanity. Since God cannot commit error, this view suggests, the bible must be without error. However, for the Catholic Church, God relies on the skills and abilities, as well as the decision-making capabilities[6] of

---

5. The quote is attributed to St. Prosper of Aquitaine in his battle with Pelagians (those who claimed salvation was achievable through human effort).

6. For example, the author of the Gospel of John admits to selecting certain stories about Jesus to include in his gospel. In the creation of his gospel the author made numerous editorial judgments. See John 20:30-31.

the human authors of scripture living and writing in particular times and places. Such reliance, in the minds of many scholars and believers alike, introduces the possibility that mistakes were made in the writing, that mistakes were made in the copying, that mistakes were made in the translating, that mistakes were made in the editing, and that time-bound truths related to the specific context of individual writers were integrated into the word of God that do not possess lasting significance for salvation.

This raises the question of what the bible actually is and from whom or what does it arise. Put another way, is the bible a divine product or a human product? Our answer to this question shapes the way we approach the bible as a source of faith, inspiration, moral wisdom, etc. Some scholars, like Marcus Borg, argue that the bible must be and is best understood as a human product.[7] Borg insists that the bible is the product of the theological reflection of two ancient communities, ancient Israel and Christianity, on their experience of God. The bible in this view is a human response to the ancient encounter with God and therefore contains the stories, perceptions, prayers, and praise of the God whom they experienced and their understanding of the human condition, the moral life, and the origin and ultimate destiny of creation. Others suggest that the bible is a blend of the divine and the human, requiring the believing community throughout history to commit to the work of trying, with integrity and faith, to discern the timeless truths of God and distinguish them from the time-bound truths of the human authors and the communities that produced them and to whom they wrote.

This is an important question for it plays a key role in how we approach fundamental questions of biblical interpretation and application. Is the prohibition against homosexuality a timeless truth of God or a time-bound truth of the human community at the time the author wrote? Do the statements about women in 1 Timothy 2:9-15 originate from the divine or are they a series of culturally conditioned statements about women and men and what constitutes a right relationship between them? Is Paul's advice in 1 Corinthians 7:32-35 regarding the freedom to focus on God enjoyed by the unmarried timeless truth or time-bound suggestion? The concern typically raised by this question is of the slippery slope variety. If I suggest a truth in the bible is time-bound and not necessary for salvation, am I undermining the credibility and necessity of the whole of scripture? Will there be those who simply accept in the bible what they like and reject what they do not

---

7. Borg, *Reading the Bible Again for the First Time*, 3-20.

like? St. Augustine once said that if you accept in the bible what you like and reject what you do not like it is not the bible in which you believe but yourself. But, it might be equally dangerous to adhere to time-bound truths out of some false obligation as a way of protecting God's timeless truths. The latter may do as much harm to our quest for God's truth as the former. For this reason, it is always important to remember that the life of the community is the appropriate setting for the reading of scripture to prevent, as far as possible, mistakes in either direction.

Interpreting the Bible

Given the complexity of the bible, a collection produced by countless authors and editors over roughly one-thousand years, emphasis is rightly placed on developing principles and approaches to interpreting the biblical literature. There are numerous types of biblical criticism that seek to understand the author's original intent and to lay the groundwork for the interpretation and contemporary application of the passage in each succeeding generation. I wish here to highlight some examples of work done to assist in the interpretation of sacred scripture. First, textual critics focus on differences between surviving copies, comparing and contrasting those differences in an effort to determine what may have been the original text. Historical criticism involves the interpretation of a biblical text in its original context involving but not limited to knowledge of customs, idioms, grammar, ancient languages, etc. Source critics try to determine and study the sources from which the biblical authors derived their information. Form criticism studies the literary forms of the biblical books to aid in their proper interpretation. For example, we do not read the comics page from the newspaper (for those of you who may actually remember what a newspaper is) with the same seriousness as we read the front page. Knowing what type of literature with which we are dealing shapes the way we approach and read it and how we can best respond to it.

Redaction criticism studies the ways in which authors shaped the information they inherited and the purpose such reshaping plays in the biblical text. This type of criticism is not focused upon the sources the biblical authors relied upon but the finished product. Canonical criticism studies the meaning of any given text or book in light of the entire biblical canon. Narrative critics concentrate on the story aspect of the bible whereas rhetorical criticism analyzes the strategies an author uses to make what is being recounted effective. Speechwriters and presenters in any context know how important using suitable material, the organization of that material, and the choice of appropriate words can be in making a presentation effective. Rhetorical critics focus on that process for the biblical authors. Studying the text as a reflection of and a response to the social and cultural settings in which the biblical book was produced is the work of the social critic. It views the text as a window into a world of competing voices and visions and how different groups with different political, economic, and religious views shaped the text to speak to their particular concerns, needs, and aspirations. Advocacy criticism is an umbrella title given to liberationist, feminist, African American, and related studies because the proponents advocate using the results of biblical scholarship to change today's social, political, or religious situation or show how the biblical passage was used to create that contemporary context. Of course, the danger of such an approach risks the imposition of twenty-first century perspectives and issues onto the ancient texts, but the blessing of this approach is its ability to enlighten our reading of scripture by asking questions that the largely white, male, European dominated academy of previous centuries never asked while providing insights never apprehended. Multiple voices at the interpretive table only enhance our understanding of the text. Lastly, it should be noted that none of these criticisms can stand alone in providing what is necessary for a robust interpretation of the biblical canon. What is necessary is using all the types of criticism available to us in a coherent and integrated way so that we might arrive at a fuller understanding of the meaning of the biblical texts. This is the work of the integration critic. The number and diversity of the work of these critics underscores the complexity of the bible and the effort required to pursue its interpretation.

Conclusion

The bible, though complex, is a central source of truth and wisdom for the Roman Catholic Church. Though it is not understood in the same way it is in the Presbyterian tradition, it is nevertheless a normative source of the encounter with God. The believer or the interested non-believer will discover in its pages the truth God desires us to know to assist us along the path to salvation. And the believer will encounter in those pages the God who inspired the ancient writers and who revealed God's self in the people and events recounted throughout the biblical literature. The complexity of the bible often finds expression in contemporary moral debates when advocates for a particular position defend that position by recourse to the biblical literature or scientific advances seem to contradict the knowledge and wisdom of the bible. But, though differences on how to understand, approach, and correctly interpret the bible will, and should, undoubtedly endure, it remains for the Catholic tradition the word of God. The Gospel of Mark begins by stating, "The beginning of the good news of Jesus Christ, the Son of God." For the Roman Catholic Church, the bible is an essential and trustworthy vehicle through which God continues to nourish believers in every age with the proclamation of the good news of what God has done for us in Jesus of Nazareth.

Chapter Two

Our Ultimate Authority

THOMAS M. TASSELMYER

The Reformed Protestant View

WHEN I FIRST STARTED attending Presbyterian churches I was surprised by the biblical knowledge of the average church member. It seemed like everyone was at least acquainted with the stories, the people, and the basic history of the Bible and almost everyone seemed to be able to quote specific Bible verses with ease. It was a little intimidating to me because, not only was I unable to quote Bible verses, I wasn't at all familiar with even the basics of the Bible. The truth is, I had never really thought about the Bible very much. When I was growing up in the Catholic church we weren't expected to know and study the Bible. Before my Presbyterian days I thought of the Bible as a resource for the professionals who worked at the church. Sure, I could have recognized the name of a few books in the Bible, but at that particular time in my life I could not have told you how many books are in it, or the difference between a Gospel, an epistle, a psalm, or where, in general, I needed to go in this collection of texts in order to even begin a search for a specific passage of Scripture. So, when I began getting involved in small group studies I became self-conscious and embarrassed by my lack of basic Bible knowledge which felt exposed when the study leader asked us to open our Bibles to a specific passage. I remember being puzzled the first time I heard a biblically astute man talking about his "life verse." I discovered he was referring to his favorite, most inspiring, life-directing passage of Scripture and I remember hoping that no one would ever ask me

Part I: Scripture

what mine was because, at that time in my life, I would have been unable to even fake an answer.

These days I am no longer surprised that the average Presbyterian knows at least a few basic Bible facts and verses because I have seen how they are steeped in it as soon as they are born. Bible stories are the source material for Sunday School classes attended by children from two to eighteen years old. Each Sunday in church adults hear expository preaching—a comprehensive verse by verse explanation of a passage of Scripture. For many churches, a week-long Vacation Bible School is the highlight of the summer. Most churches encourage and support small group Bible studies—groups of eight to twelve women and men who gather in a home to discuss the Bible, or what the Bible says about some aspect of living as a disciple of Christ. In addition to participating in a small group, these same church members might also attend a separate Bible study designed specifically for their demographic: men, women, college students, etc. In other words, Bible studies are everywhere in Presbyterian churches. But when I was growing up I only heard the Bible when a brief passage or two was read at church on Sunday morning. For my wife Laurie, however, growing up in a Protestant church in the Bible Belt of North Carolina made a huge difference.

When Laurie and I bought our first home we were living just outside of Bel Air, Maryland, and we attended the nearby Presbyterian church. The pastor of the church was a man named Eugene Peterson. We enjoyed his sermons immensely but Laurie, who was raised in the Christian Missionary Alliance Church and grounded in preaching and teaching from the King James Version of the Bible, noticed that Pastor Peterson, though quoting Scripture, was quoting it differently. Biblically illiterate at the time, I had no clue what was grabbing her attention. A short time later Pastor Peterson informed the congregation what was going on; he was in the middle of a project we now know as his famous Bible translation called The Message. At Christ Our King Presbyterian Church in Bel Air, Maryland, we were Eugene Peterson's lucky guinea pigs. The interesting thing to me was that, although Laurie initially found his paraphrasing peculiar, she had the biblical DNA—a deeply ingrained memory of Bible stories and lessons going back to her childhood—to affirm that Pastor Peterson was indeed preaching the genuine Bible.

When we moved into a new home closer to where I work, Laurie and I attended another mainline Presbyterian church. This time, however, Laurie sensed that Sunday mornings were missing something. The pastor had well-crafted and interesting talks each week, but Laurie did not always recognize them as messages grounded in the Bible. Again, I was clueless but had learned to trust the instincts of my wife. And so, although the church was very convenient, friendly, and our growing family had settled in quite nicely, without the nourishment of genuine Bible teaching Laurie began to wither spiritually. The search for a new church was on again, until we landed in a more evangelical Presbyterian church where, in classic Reformed tradition, everything, from the way the church's leadership is organized, to the weekly sermons, adult education, youth education, and weekly adult small group gatherings, is grounded in, or focused on the Bible. And yes, even I can now quote a few verses of Scripture; I even have a life verse: 1 Peter 5:10.

Authority of the Bible

All this to say, Protestants from a Reformed theological background filter everything through the Bible. The Bible is the plumb line of truth in churches where Reformed theology is followed. Build your life, or the church, on any other source of truth and you run the risk of building a shaky structure with crooked walls, corners that don't square up, and a foundation that washes away in a storm. It's the lesson Jesus was teaching in the parable of the foolish builders; "But everyone who hears these words of mine and does not put them into practice is like a foolish man who built his house on sand. The rain came down, the streams rose, and the winds blew and beat against that house, and it fell with a great crash."[1]

However, the great battle cry of the Reformers; *Sola Scriptura*, Latin for Scripture Alone, should not be confused with *Solo Scriptura*: Scripture Only. That is, Reformed theology does not teach that Scripture is the "only" source of truth. In fact, the Bible itself points to the created world as a source of truth. For example, in Paul's Letter to the Romans he makes it clear that no one can claim that truth is unattainable because "since the creation of the world God's invisible qualities—his eternal power and divine nature—have been clearly seen, being understood from what has been made, so that people are without excuse."[2] And in Psalm 19 the Bible tells us that simply gazing into the sky will lead us toward truth, "The heavens declare the glory of God; the skies proclaim the work of his hands. Day after day they pour

---

1. Matt. 7:26-27.
2. Romans 1:20.

Part I: Scripture

forth speech; night after night they reveal knowledge."[3] In fact, according to the Bible, we do not even have to go looking for some truth, it is imbedded in our consciences. "Even Gentiles, who do not have God's written law, show that they know his law when they instinctively obey it, even without having heard it. They demonstrate that God's law is written in their hearts, for their own conscience and thoughts either accuse them or tell them they are doing right."[4]

Truth, then, is all around us and impossible to avoid. It is in the conscience that each person is born with and it is proclaimed by the created world in a general revelation that provides everyone with a basic knowledge of God. But Reformed theology insists that Scripture alone is special revelation; it is the only revelation of God's truth that is infallible and authoritative in all matters of faith and practice. The Westminster Confession of Faith—which itself is considered by Presbyterians to be a source of truth because it contains a summary of Reformed theology found in the Bible—shows the high status it accords to the Bible by beginning not with God, or Christ, or salvation, but with a chapter on the doctrine of Holy Scripture. To quote from chapter one of the Westminster Confession of Faith:

> The whole purpose of God about everything pertaining to His own glory and to man's salvation, faith, and life is either explicitly stated in the Bible or may be deduced as inevitably and logically following from it. Nothing is at any time to be added to the Bible, either from new revelations of the Spirit or from traditions of men. Nevertheless, we do recognize that the inward illumination of the Spirit of God is necessary for a saving understanding of the things which are revealed in the word.[5]

It is a simple principle: everything regarding salvation, faith, and the practice of that faith is based on the special revelation found in the Bible. But it is not always an easy principle to practice because the "inward illumination of the Spirit" that the Westminster Confession says is necessary to interpret the Bible can be hard to discern, can be misunderstood, or can perhaps be missed entirely, resulting in a variety of conclusions that could lead to heated debates. So, we must have reliable principles for interpreting the Bible and we must be sure that the collection of books we call the Bible is really the Word of God.

3. Psalm 19:1-2.
4. Romans 2:14-15, NLT.
5. Kelly, McClure, and Rollinson, *The Westminster Confession of Faith*, 3.

The Bible that Protestants read is comprised of sixty-six books; thirty-nine in the Old Testament and twenty-seven in the New Testament:

Old Testament

Genesis, Exodus, Leviticus, Numbers, Deuteronomy, Joshua, Judges Ruth, 1 Samuel, 2 Samuel, 1 Kings, 2 Kings, 1 Chronicles, 2 Chronicles, Ezra, Nehemiah, Esther, Job, Psalms, Proverbs, Ecclesiastes, Song of Solomon, Isaiah, Jeremiah, Lamentations, Ezekiel, Daniel, Hosea, Joel, Amos, Obadiah, Jonah, Micah, Nahum, Habakkuk, Zephaniah, Haggai, Zechariah, Malachi

New Testament

Matthew, Mark, Luke, John, Acts, Romans, 1 Corinthians, 2 Corinthians, Galatians, Ephesians, Philippians, Colossians, 1 Thessalonians, 2 Thessalonians, 1 Timothy, 2 Timothy, Titus, Philemon, Hebrews, James, 1 Peter, 2 Peter, 1 John, 2 John, 3 John, Jude, Revelation

In the Reformed tradition these books are the canon of Scripture, from the Greek word *kanon* meaning "measuring rod," because they are regarded as the writings that were inspired by God and therefore uniquely qualified to be the authority, or measuring rod, of the church.

Inspiration, Inerrancy, and Infallibility

When Reformed theologians say that Scripture is "inspired" they mean that the words of Scripture are the very words that God breathed-out, in a supernatural way, into the minds of the Bible's forty different authors over roughly 1,500 years. When the apostle Paul writes to Timothy; "All Scripture is God-breathed and is useful for teaching, rebuking, correcting, and training in righteousness . . . ,"[6] he is making it clear that the source of all Scripture is God. This does not mean that the authors of the books in the Bible were robotically writing words that were dictated by God. The various writing skills, styles, and vocabularies that characterize the texts of Scripture make it clear that God allowed the writers He inspired to communicate His words in their own voices and personalities. Luke's Gospel has the detail and precision indicative of his background as a physician. Mark's Gospel is short and blunt, and the psalms of David are filled with emotion. But as the mind of God was revealed to the mind of the writers, God, in the person of the Holy Spirit, made sure that every single word that the authors

---

6. 2 Timothy 3:16.

of Scripture wrote was the Word of God. Or, as the apostle Peter puts it; "Above all, you must understand that no prophecy of Scripture came about by the prophet's own interpretation of things. For prophecy never had its origin in the human will, but prophets, though human, spoke from God as they were carried along by the Holy Spirit."[7]

Because Reformed theology teaches that Scripture is the inspired word of God, it necessarily concludes that it is also infallible and inerrant because God cannot mislead His people, and He does not err. And, in the Reformed tradition, the claim of infallibility is the higher standard of the two, which in my line of work, is easy to understand. I am a meteorologist and occasionally (some might say miraculously!), I make what, for all intents and purposes, is an inerrant forecast—a forecast without any noticeable errors—yet I know that even after making a flawless forecast I am still vulnerable to making a mistake in my next attempt. But, if I had God-like infallibility, my forecasts would always be error free. When we say Scripture is infallible we mean that it can never fail to teach what is perfectly correct in matters of faith and practice, that is, matters pertaining to all that Christians believe, and all that Christians are to do.

To claim that Scripture is inerrant is to claim that, in the original manuscripts, everything it teaches is true. This does not mean that the authors spelled every word correctly, used perfect grammar, or wrote about scientific things using the language and principles of science as we know them in the twenty-first century. Nor does it mean that when copies or translations of the original texts were made the scribes and translators made perfect, error-free duplications. Plus, within Scripture we find the original authors using accommodating or phenomenological language, round numbers, summarizations, and it is evident that when two writers recorded the same event they sometimes emphasized different aspects of it so that one account may seem different than the other. But when the apparent errors or contradictions are closely examined, all of them can be shown to be the result of incorrect interpretive methods, or errors made by the scribes as they made copies of the original texts. One theologian put it this way, "Inerrancy means that when all facts are known, the Scriptures in their original autographs and properly interpreted will be shown to be wholly true in everything they teach, whether that teaching has to do with doctrine, history, science, geography, geology, or other disciplines of knowledge."[8]

---

7. 2 Peter 1:20-21.

8. Feinberg in Geisler, *Inerrancy*, 265ff.

Choosing the Right Books

Interestingly, there never was a time when the church did not have a Bible. The first Christians were Jews who, like Jesus, accepted the Hebrew Scriptures as the Word of God and those texts were inherited by the church and became what Christians call the Old Testament. Greek-speaking believers in the ancient church, instead of using the plural *Biblia*—Greek for "books"—used the singular *Biblos* which means "book." In other words, the many texts of the Hebrew Scriptures were considered to be one book: the Bible.

But the list of books, or canon, of the Hebrew Scriptures used by Jews in Palestine was slightly different than the one used by Greek-speaking Jews in Alexandria, Egypt. They favored a Greek translation of the Hebrew Bible created around 250 BCE by seventy scholars known as the Septuagint (Latin for "seventy"), and it added several additional books to the Palestinian canon.

Christians in the eastern portion of the empire, close to Palestine, tended to use the shorter Palestinian canon. The early church in the western areas of the empire were more likely to be influenced by Augustine, the bishop of Hippo in North Africa, who favored the Septuagint with its longer canon. The Reformers of the sixteenth century, who aligned with Augustine on many issues, disagreed with him on this issue and concluded that the books of the Palestinian canon should be considered the church's Old Testament. It may be that the Reformers made this decision because they found no evidence that Jesus or His apostles ever quoted from the additional books found in the Septuagint, even though the apostle Paul referenced other parts of it in his letters.

The canon of the New Testament was selected and affirmed as revelation from God by church leaders over the course of the first four centuries, but in a certain sense these books were not as much selected as they were recognized and received. The canon of the New Testament came from texts that were coming into circulation as the first century churches were being established. In these churches, the Holy Spirit, dwelling in the people of God, was affirming that indeed the voice of God could be heard in certain texts. But at that time there were other books circulating in the communities as well. Luke tells us that by the time he was putting pen to parchment and recording his research about Jesus, "many"[9] had already drawn up their own accounts. The Gnostics of the first century, for example,

---

9. Luke 1:1.

produced Gospels that they claimed preserved a selection of secret teachings of Jesus. And while the Gnostics were claiming to have additions to the canon, by the second century there were also some in the church who were attempting to remove some of the books already considered part of sacred Scripture.

Around the middle of the second century the need to establish an authoritative canon was becoming clear. At about that time, Marcion, the son of a bishop and a wealthy ship-owner from Sinope on the Black Sea, began to push the gnostic idea that the God of the Old Testament was not the same as the God of the New Testament. Marcion viewed the God of the Old Testament as full of wrath, evil, and only concerned with the Jewish people, whereas the God revealed in the person of Jesus Christ was good, gracious, and full of love for all. Marcion rejected the entire Old Testament and all of the texts of the nascent New Testament that he deemed as either favoring the Jews, or contradictory to his personal views. The end result was a Marcionite bible of eleven books: a remnant of Luke's Gospel and ten letters of Paul. Marcion's bible was firmly rejected by the church in Rome and Marcion was excommunicated from the church in 144 CE, but his heretical movement was a firm warning to the church that it would eventually need to establish a canon of authoritative sacred Scripture.

The need for a canon was further exemplified around the years 156-172 CE when a man named Montanus and his two prophetesses, Prisca and Maximilla, claimed to be sent by God to prophesy in the name of the Holy Spirit with a fresh new divine revelation that superseded the Christian gospel. Speaking in a state of ecstasy they warned that to oppose what they prophesied was blasphemy against the Holy Spirit. The church was faced with either accepting that the gospel of Jesus Christ was now subordinate to the new revelations of Montanus, or it could insist that the original apostolic gospel remained at the center of Christianity and the apostolic writings were uniquely authoritative. The church chose the latter and declared the teachings of Montanus heretical. The bishops of Asia Minor excommunicated Montanus and his followers and the need for a canon became even more urgent.

Before the end of the second century the project of establishing the New Testament canon was well underway. A list of books dating to the year 190 CE—the Muratorian Canon, so-called because it was discovered by L. A. Muratori—included twenty-two of the twenty-seven books that are in the New Testament we use today. Only the books of Hebrews, James, First and Second Peter, and Third John are missing. The Muratorian Canon also includes two books not found in today's Protestant Bible: The Apocalypse of Peter and The Wisdom of Solomon. But, a canon was coming together and the process of establishing it continued into the fourth century.

In 363 CE Athanasius, the bishop of Alexandria, became the first Christian to actually use the term "canon" when referring to the Bible. His Easter letter written in 367 CE is the first formal attestation of the complete twenty-seven book canon found in our current New Testament. This twenty-seven book New Testament was affirmed at the Council of Hippo in 393 CE and at the Council of Carthage in 397 CE.

But how do we know Athanasius's canon, or the wise theologians at Hippo and Carthage included the right books? Is it possible that the early church got it wrong, that Athanasius missed a book that should be in the Bible, or put one in that should not be there? To be included in the Bible, the Reformed tradition teaches that a text must meet three criteria. First, the author must be a recognized apostle, one of those chosen by Jesus and sent by Him into the world to establish His church, and who saw the risen Christ. Or, the author could be someone sanctioned by one of the apostles. Second, the book had to have been accepted and found useful by the early church. And third, the doctrines and teachings in the book must be consistent and compatible with the doctrines and teachings in all of the other books of the canon. In Reformed theology, the death of the last apostle closed the canon. It is no longer possible to meet the criteria necessary for inclusion in the canon, so the thirty-nine books of the Palestinian canon, combined with the twenty-seven books listed in the Easter letter of Athanasius, comprise the sixty-six books of the Bible used by churches in the Reformed tradition.

Interpreting the Bible

I've heard it said that in the legal world a good prosecutor can get a grand jury to indict a ham sandwich; in theology it might be said that a wily interpreter can get the Bible to confirm just about any idea imaginable. For example, we see in the church today that some are finding new ways of interpreting what the Bible says about marriage and sexuality. With regard to these issues some theologians are now interpreting various biblical texts in a way that reaches conclusions few could have imagined just a few decades ago. When it comes to such innovative new ideas I suspect many members of Protestant churches secretly crave the finality of a papal encyclical; someplace to turn in order to find a once-for-all statement that settles a theological dispute. But in the Reformed tradition there is no such singular human authority. We must rely on the Holy Spirit to guide us as we seek to interpret the Bible accurately.

The Holy Spirit is involved in the whole biblical enterprise. Reformed theology regards the Bible as special revelation—the very Word of God revealed to several authors over many years—and those authors were inspired by the Holy Spirit to write down what God had revealed to them. Everyone can read the Bible and find some reward in doing so, but in order to fully understand the redemptive value of the Bible the Holy Spirit must illumine the mind of the reader. So, the inerrant and infallible truths of the Bible come to the believer in three steps, all of which are accomplished by the work of the Holy Spirit: 1.) Revelation: from the mind of God to the mind of the author, 2.) Inspiration: from the mind of the author to the written page, 3.) Illumination: from the written page to the mind of the reader.

Illumined by the Holy Spirit, a believer in the Reformed tradition approaches Scripture with a hermeneutic—a theory, method, or set of rules of biblical interpretation—that is based on three principles: Scripture is clear enough to be understood, Scripture interprets Scripture, and the original grammatical-historical context of Scripture must be understood. The clarity of Scripture, known as the doctrine of perspicuity, means that, while not all of Scripture is equally easy to understand, its basic message is clear enough to be grasped without requiring a graduate degree in biblical theology or any special training. The Holy Spirit did not inspire the authors of Scripture to write a confusing book. Although there are passages in the Bible that are hard to understand, or complex enough to make it hard to reach agreement on their proper interpretation, that does not negate the principle that the message of the Bible, as a whole, can be understood by any clear-thinking person who can read it or hear it.

When a passage of Scripture is difficult to understand the best source of information to help clarify its meaning is Scripture itself. This is the principle of interpretation called "the analogy of faith." This is the idea that the inspired words of one passage can further explain what the Holy Spirit inspired in another passage. This principle was derived from Paul's Letter to the Romans; "If your gift is prophesying, then prophesy in accordance with your faith,"[10] where the Greek word for "in accordance" is *analogia*, and

---

10. Romans 12:6.

thus the term analogy of faith. What Paul seems to be saying here is that anyone who has the gift of prophesy, that is, the gift of interpreting Scripture and preaching it, must avoid making up their own meaning for a passage of Scripture that cannot be objectively proven from the text itself. Instead, they must interpret and preach in accordance with "your faith," meaning "the faith" expressed throughout the whole of Scripture. The Reformers held this to be a key principle in understanding what the Bible says and they insisted that all Scripture was to be interpreted with reference to all other Scripture. This makes perfect sense if Scripture really is the Word of God, because God cannot contradict Himself. The great nineteenth century Presbyterian theologian, Charles Hodge, put it this way, "If the Scriptures be what they claim to be, the word of God, they are the work of one mind, and that mind divine. From this it follows that Scripture cannot contradict Scripture. God cannot teach in one place anything that is inconsistent with what He teaches in another. Hence Scripture must explain Scripture. If a passage admits of different interpretations, that only can be the true one which agrees with what the Bible teaches elsewhere on the same subject."[11]

Reformed theology teaches that God still speaks to us today through the words of Scripture, but acknowledges the obvious: nothing in the Bible was specifically written to any person alive today. In other words, the letters of Paul were sent to real people who gathered in first century churches; they were not sent to us. But we can, in a sense, eavesdrop on those ancient communications by reading the same letters under the illumination of the Holy Spirit. In that way we can hear the voice of God speaking not only to Christians who lived long ago, but also to us today. However, we eavesdrop with twenty-first century ears and this makes it critical to establish the historical-grammatical context of the Scripture so that we are aware of how the text was received by those who first heard it, and we understand the author's original intentions. When we approach Scripture this way, the Bible in the hands of a Spirit-filled believer can infallibly reveal God's truth bringing to light scripturally-consistent, timeless principles, applicable to the church and to individual Christians even today.

In the Reformed tradition, then, it makes sense to regard Scripture alone as the final source of authority in all matters of faith and practice, the place to turn to for answers pertaining to theology, the church, worship, prayer, discipleship, evangelizing, and countless other matters. In the Presbyterian church where I am a member, one of our core values is called

---

11. Hodge, *Systematic Theology*, Vol. 1.

Part I: Scripture

"Biblical Truth that Connects," and part of what that means is; ". . . the Bible will take first place in our lives as the lens and light by which we see, imagine and evaluate everything. We do not want to make an idol out of theology but will dig deep to hear Scripture clearly and thoroughly so we can connect its truth to people's core concerns and needs."[12] That, I believe, summarizes well the role of the Bible in churches of the Reformed tradition.

---

12. Hunt Valley Church: http://www.huntvalleychurch.org/values/ accessed January 31, 2015.

Part II

Salvation

What Does Your Church Teach is Necessary to Attain Heaven?

Chapter 3

Faith Alone

THOMAS M. TASSELMYER

The Reformed Protestant View

THE QUESTION WE ARE addressing in this chapter presumes that heaven is a place where most, if not all of us, want to eventually be. But how badly do we want it? Many of us are kept very busy in the pursuit of earthly things such as wealth, health, and physical pleasure but rarely even consider how to have "treasure in heaven."[1] It makes me wonder if the church has spent too little time helping us grasp the radical nature and awesome beauty of the biblical description of heaven. Jesus calls heaven "paradise."[2] The prophet Isaiah sees heaven as an amazing place where "the sound of weeping and of crying" will be heard no more,[3] people will not "labor in vain, nor will they bear children doomed to misfortune,"[4] and "the wolf and the lamb will feed together . . . They will neither harm nor destroy."[5] The apostle John describes heaven as a place where God dwells "among the people . . . God himself will be with them and be their God. He will wipe every tear from their eyes. There will be no more death or mourning or crying or pain, for

---

1. Matt. 19:21.
2. Luke 23:42-43.
3. Isaiah 65:19.
4. Is. 65:23.
5. Is. 65:25.

the old order of things has passed away."⁶ If heaven is truly as the Bible describes it; a place where we spend eternity in the very presence of God without a speck of useless work, misfortune, crying, pain, or death, then who would not give up everything in order to be there? And yet, as C. S. Lewis wrote in his essay *The Weight of Glory*, ". . . it would seem that Our Lord finds our desires not too strong, but too weak. We are half-hearted creatures, fooling about with drink and sex and ambition when infinite joy is offered us, like an ignorant child who wants to go on making mud pies in a slum because he cannot imagine what is meant by the offer of a holiday at the sea. We are far too easily pleased."⁷ I think Lewis is right; we have a stronger desire to stay here, even though "here" is like playing in a mud puddle compared to the infinitely more joyful place offered to us in heaven.

Perhaps because God knows our reluctance to leave the comfort of what we know for the promise of better things less known, He not only tells us what heaven is like in the Scriptures; He actually gives us glimpses of heaven here on earth. For me those God-given glimpses of heaven come in a sunrise over the beach, a trout sipping a fly from the surface of a pristine stream, a view of the Blue Ridge Mountains from the Skyline Drive, a clear glacier lake high in the Rocky Mountains, a quiet snowfall, and a newborn baby in its mother's arms. But these experiences are just temporary glimpses. The issue we are exploring in this chapter concerns how we can make these glimpses last forever, how we can enjoy heaven for eternity when we die.

In my mind the differences between Catholic and Reformed theology on this topic stem from how each tradition understands God's sovereignty, His grace, and our justification. And since in part one I emphasized Scripture as the final source of authority for Reformed theologians when it comes to matters of faith and practice, that is where I will begin my attempt to highlight the Reformed view of these doctrines. Fortunately, the Gospel of Matthew gives us a good place to start for in it we find Jesus answering the very question we are asking.

Matthew tells the story of a man who approached Jesus and asked, "Teacher, what good thing must I do to get eternal life?"⁸ This man wanted Jesus to teach him what was required of him in order to secure his place in heaven when he died. Jesus, as usual, doesn't simply answer the question,

---

6. Revelation 21:3-4.
7. Lewis, *The Weight of Glory*, 26.
8. Matt. 19:16.

He gives the man more to think about; "'Why do you ask me about what is good?' Jesus replied. 'There is only One who is good. If you want to enter life, keep the commandments.'"[9] According to Jesus, the first thing the man needs to understand is that God alone is truly good, and therefore God is the "only One" who can really *do* anything good. Second, the man is told that to have eternal life, that is, to be in heaven when you die, you must keep the commandments. Sensing, perhaps, that this is doable, the man asks Jesus to clarify so that he can be sure. "'Which ones?' he inquired."[10] Jesus rattles off five of the Ten Commandments, adds the Levitical command to love your neighbor as yourself,[11] and seems to make the man more confident, but perhaps incredulous. Is it possible that he has already met the requirements for eternal life in heaven? "'All these I have kept,' the young man said. 'What do I still lack?'"[12] Jesus then makes it very clear that the man still does not comprehend the scope of what has been described; "Jesus answered, 'If you want to be *perfect*, go, sell your possessions and give to the poor, and you will have treasure in heaven. Then come, follow me.'"[13] Note that the man never asked Jesus to tell him how to be "perfect." Rather, he asked Jesus what he lacked with regards to earning eternal life. But Jesus's answer is a clear indication that the man, whether he knows it or not, is really asking "How can I be perfect?" because being perfect is what you have to "do" to get eternal life. No wonder the man's mood changed; "When the young man heard this, he went away sad, because he had great wealth."[14]

Heaven is Not Earned

In this story we see the answer to the question of our chapter: What is required for a person to be in heaven when they die? Answer: They must be perfect. They must keep all of God's commandments and love their neighbor as much as they love themselves. The rich young man came to understand how impossible this is. I imagine him pondering in his mind whether or not he *really* kept all the commandments that he claimed to keep, and even if he did—at least in some technical sense—did he really love his poor

9. Mat. 19:17.
10. Matt. 19:18.
11. Leviticus 19:18.
12. Matt. 19:20.
13. Matt. 19:21, emphasis added.
14. Matt. 19:22.

neighbors as much as he loved himself and his possessions? This man was coming to grips with the reality of a broken world, and humanity's corrupted nature passed down from our first parents who disobeyed God in Eden.[15] Theologians call it the "Fall" and in the Reformed tradition it "completely disinclines, incapacitates, and turns us away from every good."[16] If it was now clear to this man that no matter how hard he tried, he could not be good enough to earn eternal life, then he was apparently a decent student because that is the lesson that Jesus reiterated for His disciples; "Again I tell you, it is easier for a camel to go through the eye of a needle than for someone who is rich to enter the kingdom of God.'"[17]

The fact that the disciples of Jesus were slow learners is something that we can all be thankful for because when they were confused they asked more questions—usually the questions we too would have asked—and Jesus gave more answers, which were dutifully recorded by the Gospel writers. In this case the disciples were just as astonished at what Jesus was teaching as the rich young man but, unlike him, they did not walk away from Jesus despondent. Instead they stuck around trusting there was more to what Jesus was saying.

The disciples considered material wealth a sign of God's favor and approval therefore, they reasoned, rich people are the most likely of all to spend eternity in heaven. But, if Jesus was saying that it is impossible for rich people—those who seem to have earned God's approval—to have eternal life, the disciples were desperate to know; "Who then can be saved?"[18] Jesus's answer is crucial to the question we are asking in this chapter; "Jesus looked at them and said, 'With man this is impossible, but with God all things are possible.'"[19] Jesus taught the rich young man, and His own disciples too, that it is impossible for a person to live up to the standard of perfection that God requires for eternal life: perfectly keep the commandments of God and perfectly love your neighbor as yourself. In other words, it is impossible for a person to save himself and to earn eternal life in heaven. But it is not impossible for God. If any of us are ever to experience eternity in the paradise that is heaven, it will be entirely up to God.

15. Genesis 3.
16. Westminster Confession of Faith, 6.4.
17. Matt. 19:24.
18. Matt. 19:25.
19. Matt. 19:26.

God's Sovereign Choice

The doctrine of God, and especially His sovereignty, is the linchpin of Reformed theology. All doctrines are affected by our understanding of who God is. When we say God is sovereign we understand Him to be the supreme ruler over all creation. Nothing about Him is contingent or dependent on anything in creation. His sovereignty flows naturally out of His divine attributes as revealed in Scripture. For example, He is almighty or omnipotent; no thing in creation can overpower Him, and because He has all power whatever God wills He is able to do. God is omniscient; He knows all things past, present and future. And because He has perfect wisdom, He not only knows all things, He knows precisely what to do with them. God has never made a mistake, a bad plan, or a foolish decision, He always does what is right. God is a law unto Himself, so His behavior is not contingent upon an external law or force; it is determined by His own righteous character. God acts freely and righteously according to what He is, and He works everything according to His own unchangeable and righteous will. God does not rule by referendum; the Ten Commandments are not suggestions, they express God's will. God does only what He wants to do, and since God's choices and actions are determined by His omniscience, perfect righteousness, and perfect holiness, we know that God's choices and actions are perfectly good. A high view of God's sovereignty should be very comforting to us because, as the apostle Paul said, "If God is for us, who can be against us?"[20]

So, from the Reformed perspective, God is completely sovereign over everything in the universe, including us; therefore, our salvation and whether or not we will spend eternity in heaven, cannot depend on a decision or response from us. It is contrary to God's nature to be dependent on His creatures. The psalmist tells us, "Our God is in heaven; he does whatever pleases him."[21] One of the things God does, according to the apostle Paul, is choose whom He will save. "In him we were also chosen, having been predestined according to the plan of him who works out everything in conformity with the purpose of his will, in order that we, who were the first to put our hope in Christ, might be for the praise of his glory."[22] Here we see that not only does God choose whom He will save, the people

---

20. Romans 8:31.
21. Psalm 115:3.
22. Ephesians 1:11-12.

Part II: Salvation

He chooses were "predestined" to be chosen—God had predetermined a destiny for His chosen ones. In fact, Paul tells Timothy that God had this plan in place before He made the world, and He already knew the people He would choose to spend eternity in heaven even before they ever had a chance to do anything to earn his favor: "He has saved us and called us to a holy life—not because of anything we have done but because of his own purpose and grace. This grace was given us in Christ Jesus before the beginning of time . . ."[23]

And Paul is clear that the people God chose for salvation before time began will, without a doubt, be glorified in heaven. "And those he predestined, he also called; those he called, he also justified; those he justified, he also glorified."[24] We note here that Paul does not say that *some* of those God predestined agreed to be called, or that *some* of those God called actually accepted the call and are justified, or that *some* of those God justified responded by living a good life and are finally glorified. From the Reformed perspective, this statement from the apostle indicates that the people God chooses to save have no choice in the matter; they will be glorified in heaven. As Martin Luther stated; salvation is *extra nos*: outside of us, it is entirely the work of God. The Westminster Confession of Faith puts it this way: "Before the creation of the world, according to His eternal, unchangeable plan and the hidden purpose and good pleasure of His will, God has chosen in Christ those of mankind who are predestined to life and to everlasting glory. He has done this solely out of His own mercy and love and completely to the praise of His wonderful grace. This choice was completely independent of His foresight of how His created beings would be or act. Neither their faith nor good works nor perseverance had any part in influencing His selection"[25]

Recently, I was leading a study of the Westminster Confession of Faith with a group at my church and, as is typical when Reformed theology is the topic, the discussion wound its way into the nuances between God's sovereignty and humanity's free will. We were wading through the tricky issue of God sovereignly choosing—based solely on His will—to show mercy on some but not others. Back and forth the group went, each person sharing their own thoughts, ideas, and struggles with this concept until someone finally blurted out, "Then what's the point? If the choices God makes to

---

23. 2 Timothy 1:9.
24. Romans 8:30.
25. WCF 3.5.

save people are completely independent of what we do and how we live our lives; how is that fair?" This man had reached the exact conclusion that the apostle Paul had anticipated a couple thousand years ago, "What then shall we say? Is God unjust?"[26] The fact that this question is still being asked twenty centuries later is a pretty good indication that it is a really good question. It seems natural to wonder if God is unjust when he promised eternal life in paradise to a criminal on the cross next to Jesus,[27] but allowed the rich man to walk away unsaved simply because he did not want to give away his possessions. Paul had a strong inclination that we would ask this question and he was ready for it. "What then shall we say? Is God unjust? Not at all! For he [God] says to Moses, 'I will have mercy on whom I have mercy, and I will have compassion on whom I have compassion.' It does not, therefore, depend on human desire or effort, but on God's mercy."[28] In the Reformed tradition salvation is about God's grace and mercy. Since "all have sinned and fall short of the glory of God,"[29] the fair thing for God to do is not save any of us. In such a scenario we would all be treated equally with perfect justice. But the amazing thing is that God *is* merciful, and He *does* choose to save some, even though they do not deserve it. And He makes these choices between justice and mercy according to His own perfectly righteous, wise and holy will, which is not contingent on whether we accept an invitation or respond to a call. Before the world began, God had already chosen the people on whom He would show mercy and destined them to be saved as part of His eternal plan simply because it pleased Him.

This can be hard to hear because it sounds like God has made people culpable for the sinful things they do even though they are only acting the way God himself planned for them to act from all eternity. There is great mystery here, but the apostle Paul anticipated our question. "One of you will say to me: 'Then why does God still blame us? For who is able to resist his will?' But who are you, a human being, to talk back to God? 'Shall what is formed say to the one who formed it, "Why did you make me like this?"' Does not the potter have the right to make out of the same lump of clay some pottery for special purposes and some for common use?"[30] Here Paul reminds us of God's absolute sovereignty; He is the Creator and we are the

26. Romans 9:14a.
27. Luke 23:43.
28. Romans 9:14-16.
29. Romans 3:23.
30. Romans 9:19-21.

creatures, and God has the right to create people for different purposes and with different destinies. God does this "to make the riches of his glory shine even brighter on those to whom he shows mercy, who were prepared in advance for glory."[31] Paul wants us to realize that God is not obligated to show mercy on anyone, but He does, and we should be amazed at how glorious God's mercy is.

Some will also push back against such a high view of God's sovereignty because it seems to them that God has removed our free will. If God does whatever he pleases and planned everything before time began, what is left for us to will and to choose? The Reformed tradition understands the Scriptures to say that God created humanity with a will that by nature is free. But, humans never had the ability to overrule God's sovereignty. God's freedom has always been greater than human freedom because that is how we are truly free. My friend, Andy Horvath, shared his favorite story illustrating this way of viewing real freedom. He describes a fictional playground on the roof of a high building. Children are taken to play there but the sounds of laughter and fun are missing because everyone is huddled at the center of the playground afraid of getting near the edge of the roof. However, when a high and strong fence is installed around the perimeter of the roof the children are freed to play; they run throughout the playground, kicking and throwing balls, and even banging into the fence at times while chasing after the balls. They experience real freedom even though their freedom has been limited by the fence. God's sovereignty fences in our free will, in a sense, but it also allows us to be truly free by setting the boundaries within which we experience the fullness of being human.

In the Bible we see how God's sovereignty and humanity's free will work together. The apostle Paul tells the Philippian church "continue to work out your salvation with fear and trembling, for it is God who works in you to will and to act in order to fulfill his good purpose."[32] My pastor, Frank Boswell, illustrates God's sovereignty and humanity's free will by using the analogy of a rope on a pulley. The two ends of the rope dangle through two separate holes in the ceiling. The pulley is unseen, hidden above the ceiling. One end of the rope represents God's sovereignty, the other end of the rope is our free will. We use the two ends of the rope to pull ourselves up to where God is. But if we only pull on the side of the rope that is God's sovereignty, the pulley spins and the rope falls through.

---

31. Romans 9:23, NLT.
32. Philippians 2:12-13.

The same thing happens if we only pull on the side of the rope that is our free will. But, if we hold both ends of the rope—God's sovereignty and our free will—in tension, we can pull ourselves up to where the pulley is and discover the hidden mystery of how God uses the two together. On this side of the mystery all we can really know is that we do freely make choices, but they are the choices that God ordained from all eternity, and God uses the choices of fallen people to carry out his plan.

The fall was a result of believing the lie that humanity could be completely autonomous, that is, free, self-directing gods. When the serpent tempted Adam and Eve, he said, "you will be like God."[33] Believing that lie was like believing humans could climb up to where God is with just one end of the rope, by the power of our own will. The corruption of the fall has been passed on to all of Adam's descendants so that now all of our choices are expressions of a sinful nature and we are unable to do anything spiritually good to save ourselves. "For the sinful nature is always hostile to God. It never did obey God's laws, and it never will. That's why those who are still under the control of their sinful nature can never please God."[34] But some people come to realize this truth and that realization itself is evidence of God's grace already at work in them.

God's Special Grace

In Reformed theology, grace is God's unmerited favor. God bestows common grace on everyone. For example, He holds the entire universe together through his Son,[35] He makes himself known to everyone,[36] He gives everyone a conscience and the ability to know what is right and wrong,[37] He establishes civil governments that keep the order for all people,[38] and He sends rain on both the just and the unjust.[39] These are just a few of the ways in which all people—regardless of what they do with their lives—enjoy God's benevolence.

---

33. Genesis 3:5.
34. Romans 8:7-8, NLT.
35. Colossians 1:17.
36. Romans 1:20.
37. Romans 2:14-15.
38. Romans 13:1.
39. Matt. 5:45.

PART II: SALVATION

But some people receive God's special grace—His special love for those He chose to redeem in Christ even before He made the world. "This grace was given us in Christ Jesus before the beginning of time."[40] This special grace is necessary because, as we have already noted, in a fallen world where our will is corrupted, we are enslaved to sin,[41] and we are incapable of doing anything spiritually good to save ourselves.

I like the way pastor Tommy Nelson from Denton, Texas puts it. "We need God to jiggle our willer." God's special grace "jiggles" the will of those He chose to save. It is experienced by the indwelling of the Holy Spirit. "And I will put my Spirit in you and move you to follow my decrees and be careful to keep my laws."[42] By God's special grace the wills of God's chosen ones are no longer enslaved to sin, the Spirit of God is in them, and they are brought back from spiritual death. "Because of his great love for us, God, who is rich in mercy, made us alive with Christ even when we were dead in transgressions—it is by grace you have been saved."[43] All of this is the unmerited favor and work of God. "He saved us, not because of righteous things we had done, but because of his mercy. He saved us through the washing of rebirth and renewal by the Holy Spirit."[44]

Why did the rich man walk away from Jesus feeling sad while the disciples stayed and followed him? It appears that, up to that point in his life, the rich man had only received God's common grace, which had allowed him to enjoy a life of prosperity. The disciples had received God's special grace, and the Spirit of God was moving them to follow Christ and trust Him as well.

God's Gift of Faith

The Reformers not only held to *Sola Scriptura,* Scripture Alone, as the final source of God's revealed truth. They also found within Scripture four other "*solas*" that summarized their theological beliefs regarding salvation. Salvation is *Sola Gratia*: by God's grace alone; *Sola Fide*: through faith alone, *Solus Christus*: in Christ alone; and *Soli Deo Gloria*: for the glory of God alone.

---

40. 2 Tim. 1:9.
41. John 8:34.
42. Ezekiel 36:27.
43. Ephesians 2:4-5.
44. Titus 3:5.

In the Reformed tradition God's special grace is irresistible. God does not choose people and give them His special grace so that they are empowered to decide whether they want to cooperate with Him. Whomever God has chosen will certainly be washed, renewed, and made spiritually alive by the Holy Spirit. They will receive God's gift of saving faith, and they will trust in Christ alone for salvation and eternal life in heaven.

Right after Paul reminds the church in Ephesus that without God's grace they are spiritually dead, he tells them, "For it is by grace you have been saved, through faith—and this is not from yourselves, it is the gift of God—not by works, so that no one can boast."[45] In other words, the ones that God has predestined to spend eternity in heaven cannot claim to have done anything at all. God not only chose them and made them spiritually alive, He also gave to them as a free gift, the faith that saves them. And that faith saves them because through it, God gives them *His righteousness*.[46]

So, the gift of faith is absolutely essential for salvation. It allows us to believe—or trust in—Jesus Christ, and as a result God credits us with His own righteousness. It is stunning when you contemplate it, no human would invent a plan of salvation like this! What makes you right with God is God's own righteousness credited to you, through the gift of faith that God gave you, faith in what God Himself has done for you on the cross. Clearly, then, what God has done on the cross is absolutely essential for our salvation because that is what we believe in, trust in, have faith in.

God's Sacrifice of Christ

Paul says justification—being made right with God—is given freely "by his grace through the redemption that came by Christ Jesus. God presented Christ as a sacrifice of atonement, through the shedding of his blood—to be received by faith."[47] So, our salvation is based on faith—trusting in—not the things that we do, but the things that Jesus Christ has done; His sinless life of perfect obedience to God, and His sacrificial death on the cross to make atonement for our sins.

Atonement is a word that combines "at" and "one," and it is the way in which the moral debt incurred by sin is paid to God making Him at one—reconciled with—those who have faith. We see God establishing this

---

45. Ephesians 2:8-9.
46. Romans 3:22.
47. Romans 3:24-25.

concept of atonement for Israel with the sacrifice of bulls and goats on the annual Day of Atonement. In chapter sixteen of the Book of Leviticus the high priest was instructed to sacrifice a young bull as a sin offering for himself and his household. The high priest then laid his hands on the head of a goat to transfer, or impute, the sins of the people to the goat which was then driven into the wilderness to carry the sins of the people away (a scapegoat). A second goat was sacrificed and the blood of that one was sprinkled on the "atonement cover" or lid of the ark of the covenant to atone—pay the moral debt—for the sins of the people.

But the Old Testament sacrifices were only "an annual reminder of sins;"[48] they foreshadowed the sacrifice of Jesus on the cross because it "is impossible for the blood of bulls and goats to take away sins."[49] Therefore, God presented Jesus Christ as a sacrifice of atonement because, as the sinless Son of God, He was uniquely qualified to be the "once for all"[50] sacrifice. He is the high priest without sin and therefore He did not require a sacrifice for himself. He is the Lamb of God who takes the guilt and sins of the world upon himself and carries them away.[51] And He is the one who "was pierced for our transgressions, he was crushed for our iniquities; the punishment that brought us peace was on him, and by his wounds we are healed."[52]

God's Glory Displayed

Salvation is made possible because of God's grace, God's righteousness, God's gift, and God's work; it is completely *extra nos*—outside of us. At the moment when saving faith begins a person is justified and assured of eternity in heaven all because of what God has done for them, and in them. All believers have the Holy Spirit of God living in them and by His power the response to all of this is unstoppable, and begins immediately; it is marked by a desire, and the ability, to live a life more obedient to God, a life gradually filled with more praise and worship of God. And that is precisely why God chooses to save some people, "in order that we, who were the first to put our hope in Christ, might be for the praise of his glory."[53]

48. Hebrews 10:3.
49. Hebrews 10:4.
50. Hebrews 10:10.
51. John 1:29.
52. Is. 53:5.
53. Ephesians 1:12.

But, even those whom God does not save still bring him glory. God does not condemn innocent people; everyone has sinned and owes a moral debt to God.[54] And as a good and perfect judge, God either extends mercy to the guilty, or He exercises his perfect justice and punishes them. In both cases the glory of God is displayed.

Conclusion

What is required for a person to spend eternity in heaven? I think all of Christianity would agree that the answer to this question is focused on how a person receives God's gift of salvation provided by the life, death, and resurrection of Jesus Christ. The Reformed tradition aligns with Calvin and Augustine and interprets the apostle Paul's writings regarding salvation as monergistic: God does everything. For example, Paul, quoting from the psalms says, "'There is no one righteous, not even one; there is no one who understands; there is no one who seeks God. All have turned away, they have together become worthless; there is no one who does good, not even one.'"[55] It seems difficult to conclude that salvation is synergistic—God and us together—in light of Scripture that tells us no one is even seeking God; in fact, everyone is headed in the opposite direction having turned away from God. From a Reformed perspective, salvation leading to eternity in heaven is accomplished entirely by God because people are unable to save themselves. Everyone is spiritually dead from birth and dead folks cannot do anything.

I think a good (though not perfect) illustration of the differences between our traditions is the man overboard scenario. Imagine a man who falls over the side of a ship that is cruising through the deep sea. The signal goes out for the ship to stop and a rescue crew is assembled. In the synergistic view of salvation, a life preserver is tossed on a rope to the man who fell overboard, and he paddles his way to it, holding on for dear life. The crew onboard the ship pulls him up to the deck and he is saved! Salvation for this man was accomplished through the combined efforts of his work to reach the float and hang on, and the work of the crew who threw the life preserver to him and pulled him to safety. The man had a role in the salvation that was offered to him and he even had the choice to ignore the offer made by his savior if he wanted to.

54. Romans 3:23.
55. Romans 3:10-12.

Part II: Salvation

In the monergistic view of salvation the man who fell overboard manages to stay afloat for a few minutes and then drowns; he sinks to the bottom of the ocean dead. One of the ship's crew grabs some scuba gear and jumps into the ocean to find the dead man. The scuba diver brings the dead man up to the deck of the ship and performs cardiopulmonary resuscitation (CPR) on him. Amazingly the man comes back to life; he is saved! The salvation of the man in this case was entirely up to the work of his savior. The man was dead and therefore unable to participate in any way; he could not even choose whether or not he wanted to be saved.

The illustration is not perfect; it lacks the death and resurrection of the savior, and the double imputation of the man's sins to his savior and the savior's righteousness to the man, but it shows that to be saved, to know that eternal life with God in heaven is assured, a "fallen" person needs God to jump in, grab him, and breathe new life into him. And the Bible tells us that God's CPR provides more than just air in the lungs and a pumping heart; it is the Holy Spirit who is breathed into a person in order to make them alive again, convicting them of their sins and giving them faith in the life, death, and resurrection of Christ.

The obvious question then becomes: What about life on this side of heaven? Does such a high view of God's sovereignty, a God-does-everything view of salvation, render life in this world irrelevant? This would be true only if the end of our salvation was justification. But it is not. In the Reformed tradition the moment a person is made right with God, when God's righteousness is counted as our righteousness through the faith that He gives to us, we are justified and eternity in heaven is guaranteed, but the process of salvation continues.

Justification happens at a point in time, after which, sanctification begins necessarily and immediately. In other words, sanctification—a lifelong process of gradually removing the old sinful nature and becoming more like Christ—is always evident in a person who has God's gift of saving faith. And saving faith is alive, not dead;[56] it is displayed in the way a person who has been chosen by God and destined for eternity in heaven lives their life. For these people, the fruit of the Holy Spirit who dwells in them is manifest and the world is blessed by the love, joy, peace, patience, kindness, goodness, faithfulness, gentleness, and self-control that becomes more and more characteristic of their behavior.[57] By the power of the Holy Spirit they grow

---

56. James 2:17.
57. Galatians 5:22-23.

in Christlikeness and are able to live as the apostle Paul admonished the believers in Colossae to live. They are able to "put to death" things like "lust, evil desires and greed," they rid themselves of "anger, rage, malice, slander, and filthy language," they stop lying to each other and instead they "bear with each other and forgive one another," and their hearts become filled with "the peace of Christ" and much gratitude.[58] The ability to live in this sanctified way does not earn them heaven; it is actually another glimpse of heaven here on earth, revealed for all to see by those who have been chosen by God, indwelt by the Holy Spirit, and given the gift of saving faith. These people are on-their-way, so to speak, and through the work of the Holy Spirit their sanctification will continue until their glorification immediately after death, when the soul is made perfectly holy and they enjoy the presence of God in heaven for eternity.

---

58. Col. 3:1-17.

Chapter 4

Heaven

The Fulfillment of a Relationship

Lyle K. Weiss

When I was a young boy, I can remember looking skyward to the clouds as they floated lazily across the bright blue sky. Springtime was a particularly rich time for heaven gazing. The season of Lent, the period of forty days leading up to and preparing for the celebration of Christ's death and resurrection, always made me feel a bit closer to God than normal and looking up at the clouds, I could almost see the savior who promised that one day we would see him coming on the clouds of heaven. Nowadays, I must admit I do not live from a vision of the Lord's imminent return, though I sometimes assume he will decide to reveal himself the morning after I finally win the Powerball jackpot. But, looking heavenward as a young man, often left me pondering a wide range of questions. The concept of heaven was always too much for my young mind to grasp. How could we live forever? The notion of forever was simply beyond me. And what would we do forever? The length of the school day was too much for me. Hanging out with angels singing the same boring hymns we had to sing during mass did not strike me as a particularly exciting way to spend eternity. During my teen years, I found myself agreeing with Billy Joel when he sang that he would rather "laugh with the sinners than cry with the saints. The sinners are much more fun." True, my theological understanding of the notion of heaven would change and grow as the years passed. At that point in my development though, I had a very underdeveloped vision of the beauty of heaven and its profound significance as both a goal and a mission. But, I still pondered it, wondered about it, and hoped one day I might be lucky enough to live in it.

Defining Heaven

In order to outline what the Catholic tradition believes about heaven and entrance into it, it might be helpful to begin by clarifying what is meant by the term heaven. Too often, we think of heaven as a place we go to in the aftermath of death. The New Testament vision, as N.T. Wright has correctly articulated it, understands the fulfillment of God's kingdom as the marriage of heaven and earth.[1] Just as Jesus' crucified, human body is transformed into a newly embodied form of everlasting existence, so too will earth be finally transformed into a new state of eternal existence in which God will reign forever. Location aside, the question this chapter asks is how can a person be included in the marriage of the new heaven and new earth, living with and in God forever? In this chapter, I will use the term heaven as a shorthand for expressing this understanding of the fulfillment of God's saving design as the marriage of the new heaven and new earth rather than speaking of heaven as a place to which we go when we die. In the sense of the marriage of heaven and earth, heaven is a term used by the Christian tradition to refer to the perfect communion in life and love with the most Holy Trinity. At its core, the language of heaven is fundamentally about union with God. But, it is also about union with all those who are in Christ. I can recall various conversations through the years during which my friends and I pondered the identities of the people we would most like to meet and talk with should we ever be fortunate enough to enjoy heavenly communion. Those conversations were always fun, offering insight into our distinct personalities based upon the substance of the lists we formulated. But, and far more personally, in addition to meeting famous people from history, we believed we could also take consolation in the possibility of meeting our friends and loved ones from whom we are currently separated through death. Those of us who have lost dearly cherished loved ones share in the hope of that longed for heavenly reunion. So, the anticipation of heavenly citizenship brings with it not only the expectation of seeing God face to face and the joy of living in God's love forever in a transformed heaven and earth but the happiness that will surely be ours when reunited

1. Wright, *Surprised by Hope*, 104-105.

with loved ones and sharing in the blessed opportunity to meet others who have traversed our mortal path throughout the centuries. Understood in terms of eternal union with God and others, in the Roman Catholic vision, heaven is not understood as a reward given to an individual for a life well lived but rather articulates a communal vision of those who are with Christ but are also in Christ.

St. Paul assures us that, should our earthly dwelling be destroyed, "we have a building from God, a dwelling not made with hands, eternal in heaven."[2] During his final meal with the disciples in John's gospel, Jesus assures his disciples that he will return to take them to his Father's house. "And if I go and prepare a place for you, I will come back again and take you to myself, so that where I am you also may be."[3] In the beginning of the Acts of the Apostles, Jesus is ascending until a cloud takes him from their sight. The disciples are staring heavenward when two men in white clothes appear beside them and ask, "Men of Galilee, why are you standing there looking at the sky? This Jesus who has been taken up from you into heaven will return in the same way as you have seen him going into heaven."[4] We see the same theme of Christ's return to be with us always in Paul's First Letter to the Thessalonians when Paul envisions the future return of Christ, concluding with the hope-filled promise that "we shall always be with the Lord."[5] According to the authors of the New Testament, humanity's ultimate destiny is to live forever with God in Christ through the Spirit.

Leading the Gospel Life

Every book of the New Testament in some way speaks of the future awaiting those who have faith in Christ and live according to the gospel he proclaimed. Matthew's vision of the final judgment commends those who acted justly and rightly towards the least of Jesus' brothers and sisters. They are welcomed into the kingdom of his Father, reminding them that "whatever you did for one of these least ones of mine, you did for me."[6] And a warning is given to those for whom the words, "Lord, Lord," fall easily

---

2. 2 Corinthians 5:1.
3. John 14:3.
4. Acts of the Apostles 1:11.
5. 1 Thessalonians 4:17.
6. Matt. 25:40.

from the lips but fail to do the will of Jesus' Father in heaven.[7] Arguably, the Gospel of John places upon the believer the highest burden, the highest call, and the highest honor of any book of the New Testament when, on the night before he dies, Jesus presents his disciples with a new commandment, to "love one another as I love you."[8] Famously, the author of the Letter of James proclaims that "faith of itself, if it does not have works, is dead.[9]" Earlier in the letter, the author exhorts his readers to be doers of the word, an admonition similar to the words on Jesus' lips in the gospel of Luke when a woman calls out from the crowd to bless his mother. In response, Jesus says, "Rather, blessed are those who hear the word of God and observe it."[10] Our future perfected union with God is bound up with faith in Jesus and a willingness to follow in his footsteps, doing the things he did and living from the commands he offered. He could command us to love one another because that was what he did throughout his life, exhibited in his death, and revealed through his resurrection and it is what he expects of those who follow him.

Humanity and Salvation

The answer to one question that has divided Protestants and Catholics through the centuries involves the role played, or not played, by human action in the process of determining inclusion in God's saving design. It is important to recognize this is not a question of whether we are called to live gospel lives. In my experience the most popular misconception Catholics maintain about Protestant thought and life is the belief that the moral life is unimportant for Protestants. All that matters to Protestants, in this Catholic misconception, is that you say you have faith. Saying you have faith is all that is necessary for salvation and that the way you live does not matter. It seems to me this view is only partially correct in that it rightly asserts that the substance of our lives, in the Protestant view, is irrelevant to our salvation. We are called to lead gospel lives but it remains God, and God alone, who saves regardless of the quality of our lives. To believe that the quality of our lives has some role to play in salvation would suggest that it is not God and God alone who saves but some blend of God's grace and human

7. Matt. 7:21-23.
8. John 15:12.
9. James 2:17.
10. Luke 11:28.

activity. What the popular Catholic misconception gets wrong is the second assertion expressing the belief that the moral life is unimportant to our Protestant sisters and brothers. Protestants believe firmly in the importance of responding to God's call with a life of faith and love and a commitment to justice and dignity.

The great reformer Martin Luther makes the point powerfully. He taught that if we believe the quality of our life makes a difference in our salvation then when we love our neighbor our love for them is not pure. Why? We love them, at least in part, because of what they obtain for us. I love them, at least in part, because by loving them I participate in earning my salvation. Put another way, every good deed I perform will be shaped by an ulterior, even if subtle, motive. Through you, I earn my salvation. The other person, therefore, can too easily and even subtly become a means to my end of salvation. I care for you not for you but for myself. For Luther, it is God alone who saves. But, that does not absolve us from living the gospel life. Rather, it frees us to live that life knowing that when I love my neighbor I do so, not because of what my neighbor provides me, but from a genuine desire to promote the well-being of my neighbor. The Christian moral life is irrelevant to salvation which is the action of God and God alone. But, living the gospel life to which we are called is central to authentic Christian faith. Not to oversimplify the point but it might be fairly said that for Protestants, the moral life flows from the reality of being saved whereas for Roman Catholics the moral life is a necessary and integral dimension of the process of being saved.

The Roman Catholic view of salvation involves two fundamental, necessary actors and components. The actors are God and the human person seeking to be saved, or rather, seeking to be united with God and all who are in Christ forever. (We must remember that salvation is not an isolated reality involving only the person but is a communal reality bound up with the entire created order.) The components are the gifts of God's grace and the human response to that gift. St. Anselm, around the year 1099, wrote a seminal book on the gift of salvation entitled 'Cur Deus Homo?' or 'Why the God Man?'[11] In Christian reflection on the central role of Christ in salvation, theologians have affirmed the notion that Jesus needed to be both divine and human in order to affect salvation because only as divine could he represent God's power to save while simultaneously representing humanity's affirmation of that gift. In the divine and human Jesus we have

---

11. Anselm of Canterbury, *Cur Deus Homo?*

both the offer and the acceptance of the offer of salvation. If Jesus were not God he could not accomplish our salvation; if Jesus were not human than what he accomplishes would be irrelevant to us. The Catholic view of heaven follows along similar lines of thought. It is not just the offer of salvation or grace alone that achieves salvation but the combination of God's saving grace and the affirmative response to that gift from human beings that achieves salvation. Like Jesus' humanity and divinity, both are necessary. Only God can extend the offer and have the power to make the offer a reality and only humanity can respond to that offer. God cannot say yes for us. This not a diminution of the role of God in salvation as much as an affirmation of the gift of freedom bestowed upon us and the key role it plays in God's saving design. Heaven is only possible because of the gift of God's grace so it is appropriate to claim that God alone can save. But, it would be an irrelevant offer if it did not involve an affirmative response from human beings. Like love, salvation is always given freely but it must also and only be responded to freely.

I have in the past tried to describe the Catholic approach using the image of the Christmas tie. Each year, dads across the country receive ties as gifts from loved ones for Christmas. Just because we receive the gift does not guarantee that we will use the gift. Undoubtedly, shoved way back in closets around the nation are ties received at Christmas that have not seen the light of day since that wonderful winter morning when the gift was first received and opened. Other dads wear their ties with pride showing off to the world the Santa tie, the reindeer tie, the Christmas tree tie, or any other holiday theme that can decorate a tie. If the tie lights up, so much the better. But, any gift received can be left unopened and unused, meaningless in the life of the receiver, regardless of the thought and the love that went into the selection of the gift. The true significance of the gift finds expression not only in its being received but in its being used. For Roman Catholicism, the gift of God's grace can be hidden away in a closet, unused and meaningless or it can be received with joy, used and displayed in such a way that it reveals the bond of love uniting the giver and receiver.

The point can also be made if we think of heaven in relational terms. We reach out to others throughout the course of our lives, offering to them our hand in friendship, support, or love. We do so in the hope that our offer will be received, accepted, and responded to in the affirmative. Although not every offer we extend is reciprocated, we nonetheless hope that some will accept our offer of friendship, that some will accept our offer of support and assistance, and that some will accept our offer of love. Not everyone whose path we cross in life will end up becoming our friend, but some will. If we reach out to support the poor or the homeless, we hope that our support might assist them in finding a new path in life. We may invite that someone special to share life with us in marriage, a desire we hope is one they share with us. It is an invitation to love we offer to our children, nurturing them, supporting them, and growing with them throughout life. Though not always reciprocated, the offer desires such reciprocation and true human fulfillment is only made possible through such reciprocation. God's grace is the extension of an invitation to unite in the bond of love, an invitation that experiences its fulfillment in the acceptance of that invitation and the creation of that union. The author of the First Letter of John, in one of the most astounding and underappreciated verses of the entire bible, writes, "if we love one another, God lives in us, and his love is brought to perfection in us."[12]

In that sense, life with God in the married heaven and earth is the fulfillment of the work of a mutual relationship. Heaven will always be dependent upon God because only God can extend the offer and has the power to make the offer a reality. So, in that sense it is true that only God can save. But, in order for that offer to experience fulfillment, the human addressee must respond affirmatively. To affirm that humanity has a role in salvation is not to diminish the unique and necessary role of God or to suggest that heaven is a destination that humanity earns or merits if you think of merit in terms of reward. But, to neglect the role humanity rightfully plays in the saving relationship risks making the human community irrelevant to salvation, that the notion of salvation as an expression of God's relationship with creation is greatly impoverished. When humanity's role is neglected salvation can be understood as a gift that God offers and that God receives and accepts, leaving little or no room for human agency, one of the greatest gifts God has bestowed upon us. Roman Catholicism seeks to balance our dependence on God for salvation with the important role we play in the saving drama. The substance of the life we lead is not an effort to earn or merit heaven. The life we lead represents our response to the gracious and generous offer of God to share in God's life forever. Only God can make such an offer, only God can transform the offer into lived reality, but only we can accept that offer, an acceptance that finds expression in our growth in faith and goodness throughout the course of our lives.

12. 1 John 4:12.

Sin and Grace[13]

The Christian tradition has been bound up with this question in its discussions of sin, grace, and salvation, discussions that have occupied it since its inception. At the heart of the biblical narrative is the conviction that God has chosen to enter into a covenant with the created order generally and humanity specifically. In fact, the biblical story can be read as a history of God's decision to enter into or renew the covenant with the ancient communities of faith. Creation itself represents a foundational covenant built upon by later covenants. Successive covenants are made with the people through Noah, Abraham, Moses, and David. At the heart of each covenant is God's call to ancient Israel to be holy. The Torah sets down for the believing community the rules and regulations that should govern the boundaries of a life lived in right relationship with God and others. It is within this covenantal history that the earliest Christians understood Jesus' death on the cross. The covenant established in and through the body and blood of Christ draws upon the symbolic significance of the prior covenants as God's response to human sin, seeing Jesus' death as the sacrificial offering through which sin is forgiven and reconciliation with God is achieved.

The Gospels of Matthew and John in particular stress the sacrificial significance of Jesus' death. The words of institution at the Last Supper in Matthew's gospel reflect this sacrificial significance when Jesus proclaims that his blood will be the blood of the new covenant to be poured out for the forgiveness of sins.[14] John makes the point, albeit in a subtler fashion. In John's gospel Jesus is crucified at noon on the Day of Preparation.[15] It is at noon on the day of preparation that the lambs to be used for the Passover meal are slaughtered. Jesus, previously identified in the gospel as the Lamb of God by John the Baptist,[16] is the lamb whose blood will bring freedom and redemption. As Jesus hangs on the cross, he says, "I thirst." In response, they place a sponge soaked in wine on a sprig of hyssop and lift it to his mouth.[17] It was with sprigs of hyssop that the ancient Hebrews smeared their doors with the blood of the lamb during the time of enslavement in

---

13. In this section, I rely heavily on Haight, S.J., *The Experience and Language of Grace.*
14. Matt. 26:27-28.
15. John 19:14.
16. John 1:29.
17. John 19:29.

Egypt so that the angel of death might pass over their homes.[18] Jesus is the new lamb whose blood will liberate a people enslaved by sin and lead them into the freedom of new life.

That covenantal narrative provides the basic structure for the Roman Catholic understanding of salvation. In each instance, it is God who initiates the covenant to which humans are called to respond. But, readers of the bible know that the relationship between God and God's people typically followed a four-stage process of development: God establishes the covenant, humanity violates the covenant, there is a consequence flowing from the violation, and lastly God renews the covenant. The establishment of the covenant is not the end of the story but the beginning. The source of sin, of covenant violation, in the bible is linked to two impulses within the human person, the yester ha-ra and the yester ha-tov, the inclination to do evil and to do good respectively. It is sin, or the surrender to the impulse to do evil, that causes the disruption in the relationship between God and God's people. Whether one perceives that disruption as the result of a primordial fall or simply the consequence of human freedom need not detain us here. For our purposes I want only to highlight that God desires union with us but through sin we have rejected that union. Only through the offer of God's grace is the attainment of such a union possible.

But, what does grace do for us and within us that allows us to experience eternal union in God with others? For Augustine, he understood the gift of God's grace within the context of human sin. The fundamental or original sin in Augustine's view actually changes human nature so that it is no longer capable of doing the good even if it wants to do the good. As St. Paul had written in his Letter to the Romans,[19] Augustine found himself doing the things he did not want to do and not doing the things he wanted to do. For Augustine, original sin so damages human nature that it is only through the assistance of divine aid, or the healing power of grace, that we are capable of doing the good. His approach, sometimes referred to as a medicinal view of grace, suggests that sin so harms human nature that we become incapable of doing the good and only through God's grace do we receive the healing necessary to allow us to do the good again.

In succeeding centuries, theologians continued to reflect on Augustine's theology of sin and grace at a time when the west was rediscovering the thought of Aristotle. In particular, Aristotle's argument from function

---

18. Exodus 12:22.
19. Romans 7:15.

helped to shape reflection on the dynamic between sin and grace. Aristotle's argument was a teleological one from the word telos or end. Put simply, Aristotle argued that what makes a thing good is related to the end for which that thing has been created. A pen is a good pen when it writes, a chair is a good chair when it supports the weight of the person sitting in it, or a car is a good car when it gets me where I need to go and back consistently. The great theologian Thomas Aquinas, grounded in Aristotle's argument, maintained that the end or goal for which humans are created is friendship with God. But, God is infinitely above humanity. Therefore, the end for which humans exist, union with God in knowledge and love, is supernatural in relation to human being and nature. That is, it is a goal beyond our human nature to achieve on its own. Human beings need a new and higher nature in order to achieve the supernatural end to which we are ordered and for which we exist. The gift we receive from God that elevates our nature to achieve our supernatural end is grace. Aquinas' thought led to a fundamental shift in the theology of grace. Grace was not necessary because of sin but because of the limitations of human nature. Grace was necessary to elevate human nature so that we might fulfill the purpose for which we are created.

An important aspect of Aquinas' thought on grace involved Aristotle's notion of habit, a notion Aquinas adopted. For both Aristotle and Aquinas, a virtue is a habit, an interior disposition or permanent quality of the soul. These internal dispositions are principles of action. Each human act is performed through some internal principle. Therefore, when I perform an act it is truly me who acts. This is true for Aquinas even when talking about God acting through me. My actions flow from some internal principle otherwise God would not need my cooperation to act through me. It would just be God acting, making me unnecessary to the action and my freedom would be compromised by God. Aquinas' notion of habit supports the claim that my acts must always be free acts, even when we speak of God acting through me. When we speak of God loving others through me, the love offered is always an embodiment of human and divine love. So, what is the relationship between grace, virtue, and the good we do? For Aquinas, grace is a habit poured into the human soul by God and as such is a permanent state, quality, or disposition. Grace is our new nature oriented to our supernatural end in God. Though it does not entirely lose the medicinal qualities grace possessed for Augustine, Aquinas nevertheless affirms that grace's primary mission is to elevate human nature so it may attain its supernatural end of union with God.

The great reformer Martin Luther rejected the dry, stale language of Aquinas' scholasticism, choosing to embrace a more personal and experiential language to articulate his view of the greatness of God and the smallness of the human person. Favoring Augustine's more medicinal view of grace, Luther saw human beings as simul justus et peccator, simultaneously sinner and redeemed. For Luther, we are justified, or forgiven of sin, through faith alone. Faith is not an act or work but surrender and a reception that renounces all claims to self-justification. Aquinas had defended the role of human merit for three reasons. First, he wanted to affirm human freedom. Second, he wanted to protect God's justice. Third, he wanted to affirm the process of exitus-reditus which claims that grace works through the human person, finding articulation and actualization in acts that move a person towards salvation. For Luther, grace was God's unmerited favor. The danger of the Catholic view, heavily influenced by Aquinas, is that it risks sliding into a legalism in which the person understands grace as a reward for living a good life and salvation as earned through that life, a view I suspect is held by many Roman Catholics today.

In contrast, Luther affirms our absolute dependence on God for salvation both before and after our conversion to Christ. But, his view risks creating a dualism that compartmentalizes a person's inner and outer life, causing a rupture or divide between a person's interior life and what they do in the world. It also makes human freedom all but disappear. Grace is God's gift that we accept in faith, which is also God's gift to us. God freely accepts God's own offer of salvation. But, one is left to wonder where the human person is in this process and what role, if any, humanity plays in its own acceptance of God's saving offer. We have probably all had the experience of being involved in a conversation that does not seem to require our presence. Our inner voice asks, "Do I need to be here for this?" Luther risks turning salvation into a conversation for which we do not need to be present. Critics rightly raise the concern that Luther's view limits humanity's role and makes grace a purely extrinsic reality. Second, Luther refers to surrender to grace as if surrender and renunciation are not human acts. Surrender and renunciation suggest a certain degree of human cooperation in the dynamic of God's grace and salvation. Finally, another critique of Luther finds expression in particular in our day and age when there exists a great deal more acceptance of the possibility of salvation outside the strict confines of Christianity's borders. Critics suggest that Luther's view of grace and salvation is too closely aligned with specific knowledge of Christianity whereas Aquinas' view has been used more recently to develop positions that support the salvation of non-Christians.[20]

The Council of Trent, Roman Catholicism's response to the reformers, affirms what God does for the human person and what the human person can do under the power of grace. For Trent, human beings cannot be justified by the power of nature. Justification involves a real remission of sin but also involves a real, interior renovation of the person. The justified person becomes a new living being enjoying a new life. Trent teaches that the process of justification involves a free acceptance on the part of the person, who is active and cooperates with God's grace. Since a person's free will is not destroyed by sin, grace moves within them through their free assent. This movement begins with God's call or what is referred to as prevenient grace. This is the call that awakens the person to God's love and mercy and to which the human person freely responds, keeping open the possibility of accepting or rejecting grace.

These assertions reject two aspects of Luther's theology of grace, the passivity of the human person in the process of justification and a particular way of understanding the doctrine of sola fide (faith alone) as being practically synonymous with sola gratia (grace alone) which, in the Catholic view, places too little stress on the other two theological virtues of hope and love, of which Paul claimed love was the still more excellent way.[21] Other claims made by Trent included the rejection of the notion that a person could possess certitude regarding the state of grace or salvation. The corollary in our day then would be a rejection of the certitude Christians claim when they declare themselves saved. In addition, Trent affirmed that it was both possible and necessary to obey the law in the belief that justice in a person increases through a faith that plays itself out in a life of good works. This contradicted Luther's claim that justice came all at once as opposed to the more gradual view of Roman Catholicism. This difference is still experienced in the Catholic notion of conversion as a gradual process played out through the course of one's life and the more evangelical view that identifies the moment at which one became saved. In summary, Trent offered the nu-

---

20. The Jesuit theologian Karl Rahner has argued a position referred to as anonymous Christianity. Though also problematic, it is nevertheless an attempt to speak of salvation outside the strict confines of membership in the Christian church.

21. 1 Corinthians 12:31.

anced thought that a believer merits salvation through good works under the power of grace. This teaching anticipated the more relational views of grace and salvation developed in the 20th and 21st centuries.

The Protestant Reformation and the Council of Trent stood on the cusp of major changes in human history. The world was moving away from revelation and church teaching as the central sources of knowledge and moving toward verifiable hypotheses and the power of reason reflecting on existence as the primary sources of knowledge. New approaches to scripture developed. No longer was scripture the infallible source of all knowledge but a literary text that could be analyzed like all other literary texts. The church, too, was no longer the source of all wisdom and truth as the Enlightenment championed the human ability to reason and placed increased emphasis on internal rather than external forms of authority. In the twentieth century, in this vastly different theological landscape, the Roman Catholic theologian Karl Rahner again took up the task of developing a theology of grace.

Augustine had understood from personal experience the power of sin in human existence, a power that inhibited human freedom. Grace was necessary to heal the wounded human heart and will, not only giving freedom to make decisions but granting liberty understood as the freedom to choose the good. Aquinas believed human nature was created good but that humanity was created with a supernatural end which human nature was incapable of fulfilling. Grace was the gift of God that elevated human nature to the level of supernature so that it could fulfill its end of union with God. Luther understood that humanity was so depraved it could not merit the gift of God's grace. Believing there was no such thing as merit or the possibility of being justified based upon our actions, he taught that it was only through unmerited grace that we are made right with God. For Trent, grace is a gift of God to which humans are called to respond. Thinking that Luther's system made the human person superfluous to salvation, the council fathers understood grace in a reciprocal way involving God's invitation and humanity's free response. Building on Trent's rejection of Luther's extrinsic view of grace, the Jesuit Karl Rahner taught that grace is intrinsic to the human person. By this he meant that grace is built into the very structure of our being, creating us with a fundamental openness to God and God's call extended to us through the presence and love of the indwelling Trinity both within us and within history. Grace is not an external force that changes the human person but an internal reality that is constitutive of who we are as human beings. To respond to the gift of God's grace requires that we become who we are created and called to be.

Social Grace

One final development to consider involves the growth of our awareness of the power of social structures in human development and our nature as social creatures. Particularly in the latter half of the twentieth century and beyond, liberation theology has examined the doctrine of grace through the lens of human liberation. Criticizing much of the history of the theology of grace for being too focused on the individual and paying insufficient attention to the social dynamism of human existence, liberation theologians developed a theology of grace that understood justification as involving God's forgiveness and mercy in a way that paid adequate attention to both the personal and social levels of human existence. Christianity maintains with the bible that human beings are created in the image and likeness of God. But, the Christian God is a Trinity of persons. God in God's very self is social. To be human therefore is to be a social being. We are saved just as we come to be; not as individual, isolated human beings but through relationships, through community life, through social existence.

In response to the critique of Karl Marx that religion was the opiate of the people by dulling them into passivity through promises of a better life to come after death, Christianity has developed a theology of God's grace operative in history. Grace is not just concerned with post-mortem existence but with the whole of human life. As Rahner once stated, eternity begins in history. How is God's grace active in human history? Grace is not just a personal reality freeing us from sin, fear, despair, and death and freeing us for life, fulfillment, happiness, justice, hope, and love. It is also a profoundly social reality calling institutions, organizations, structures, and systems out of fear and into justice and peace. The experience of sin is not just a personal reality but a social reality as well. So too, grace is not just a personal reality but a social reality. Sin touches every institution, organization, community, or structure we develop. As human beings, we are all caught in the web of social sin and so all bear some level of responsibility for social sin just as all need to be liberated from it. To be liberated by grace is to be freed to live a life consistent with the gift we have been given in Christ. As the First Letter of John states, we love because God first loved us. But, God's love is brought to perfection in us.[22] Through love, we cooperate with the Spirit of God in the transformation of the world. Whenever the human person cooperates with God's grace, that cooperation finds embodiment in human history. God acts in history through human freedom, goodness, and love to advance the cause of the kingdom proclaimed in word and deed by Jesus of Nazareth. And just as social sin finds expression in institutions and communal life, so too can grace become institutionalized, promoting human dignity, peace and justice, embodying love active in history.

Conclusion

From a Roman Catholic perspective, how do we get to heaven? How do we live forever united with God and all of the created order in love and peace in the married heaven and earth? Much can and should be said about a proper understanding of the reality of heaven. For a clear discussion, I do encourage reading N.T. Wright. But, for our purposes, it should be remembered that heaven is not simply referring to our post-mortem existence but the perfect and purified state of existence with and in God that has its roots in our current living. Our eternal union with God depends on the fundamental invitation of God to be united with him. But, it is an invitation to which humanity is called to respond, a response that finds expression in its historical embodiment in our following in the footsteps of Jesus. Grace is the necessary gift of God given to us in the very act of creation and that forms the fundamental structure of who we are as human beings. The challenge for believers and the believing community is to live shaped by God's gift, discovering in heaven the fulfillment of the personal and social life to which we have dedicated ourselves and which we have striven to embody under the power and influence of God's saving grace.

---

22. 1 John 4:10-12.

Part III

Sacraments

What are the Sacraments in Your Church and What Do They Do?

Chapter 5

Sacraments and the Continuing Mission of Jesus Christ

Lyle K. Weiss

Christianity as an Incarnational Faith

The foundational, though not perhaps the most critical, Christian belief is that God took on human flesh in the person of Jesus of Nazareth. The Incarnation, God becoming human in Jesus, is the seminal event from which all subsequent Christian history flows. Through the centuries Christian faith has reflected on the significance of the Incarnation for salvation, for the moral life, for the structure of the church, and for insight into God's immeasurable love for all creation. In this chapter, we will focus on the significance of the Incarnation for the liturgical, or more specific, sacramental life of the church. That God chose to become human, to become like one of us in all things save sin, not only reveals the depths of God's love and the profundity of God's character but it also affirms the fundamental framework of Christian identity and life. In the sacred narrative we share with our Jewish sisters and brothers, God provides his people with the law, embodied in the tablets Moses brings down from the summit of Mt. Sinai. In the New Testament, God no longer simply provides the law but his very self. Jesus is the living embodiment of the ancient law, the living embodiment of God's ancient promises, the living embodiment of God's reign, the living embodiment of the Father's love, and the living embodiment of the fulfillment towards which God is calling all of creation. The Incarnation proclaims the basic Christian truth that God's love is not floating somewhere in the atmosphere like the shimmering image of a ghost. Rather, God's love finds concrete embodiment within the arena of history. A vital expression of that concrete embodiment is the continuation of Jesus' ministry through the sacraments of the church.

Humans as Historical Beings

Humans exist within the bounds of history. Despite the heights to which our spirits might soar, we remain nevertheless embodied spirits existing within the boundaries of time and space. It is through our bodies that we interact with the world around us. Though love is a decidedly spiritual reality, we express love through a tender glance, a warm touch, a helping hand, a coy smile, or the softness of a kiss. Even though our values can be articulated in complex philosophical language, they take very concrete shape in the behaviors that realize those values in a specific time and place among specific people. As human beings, we can contemplate the angelic realms but we need food and drink to nourish us, a roof to shelter us, medicine to help heal us, a purpose in life to guide and inspire us, and human love to fulfill us. And although God can visit us within the depths of meditation and contemplation, God comes to us primarily through the concrete, the embodied, through the incarnation of his presence in the world of people and objects that swirl around us.

Jesus of Nazareth is the great incarnation of God's love, the concrete, historical embodiment of the love of God. From our own experience we know that it is easy to profess love. But, the truth of our proclamation is embodied in the myriad forms of concrete expression that love, if it is genuine, takes. This is true for all of our commitments and professed values in life. We can state our value, our commitment, or our belief, but it is easy to articulate empty words. What provides those words with truth is the extent to which our actions support our claims. I may profess to be a follower of Jesus Christ but if the substance of my life seems devoid of a forgiving and charitable spirit, if I fail to reach out to others in service and compassion, if I neglect my responsibilities as a citizen, and if I fail to participate meaningfully in the faith community, in short if my life seems absent of all the attributes of a follower of Jesus, then it is time that I examine my discipleship and draw closer to the Lord and the path of holiness to which he calls each of us.

In the Letter of James, the author speaks of the need to put our faith into practice. Though the Letter of James is a highly controversial expression of the New Testament witness regarding the relationship between faith and works, the author nevertheless makes clear that in his judgment a profession of faith without the corresponding life shaped by that profession is meaningless. It is a frank expression of the reality that words can be easy for humans to utter but difficult to embody. "What good is it," the author asks, "if you say you have faith but do not have works? Can faith save you?" The author cites examples about our responsibilities to the hungry and naked concluding, "So faith by itself, if it has no works, is dead."[1] The concept of embodied faith is at the heart of the Catholic Church's understanding of the sacraments. The church recognizes that, at the heart of our faith, we discover God's embodied love in the person of Jesus of Nazareth. The church is called to continue to embody Jesus' presence and love in the world by continuing in a concrete, historical way the mission and ministry of Jesus in its own identity and life.

Sacraments, The Ministry of Jesus, and the Mission of the Church

While in prison, John the Baptist sent messengers to Jesus to ask if he was the one who is to come or if they should wait for another. Jesus replied not by claiming the mantle of the messiah. Rather, he told John's disciples, "Go and tell John what you hear and see: the blind regain their sight, the lame walk, lepers are cleansed, the deaf hear, the dead are raised, and the poor have the good news proclaimed to them. And blessed is the one who takes no offense at me."[2] Central to Jesus' public ministry was his proclamation of the kingdom, a kingdom he believed was being established in and through his person and mission. Jesus proclaimed that kingdom in both words and deeds. In fact, his deeds and his acts of power, oftentimes referred to as miracles, were the embodied proclamation of the good news of God's coming kingdom. How did the good news of the kingdom find embodiment in Jesus' ministry? Table fellowship, healing of the sick, forgiving sinners, reconciling people with the community, raising the dead, and proclaiming the good news. All the activities Jesus cited in his answer to the messengers of John the Baptist

1. James 2:14-17.
2. Matt. 11:2-6.

and more were among the ways in which the kingdom was being realized in the life and ministry of Jesus of Nazareth.

Those who believed in Jesus, who witnessed his proclamation of the kingdom in word and deed, who received appearances of the risen Jesus after his death on the cross and his resurrection on Easter Sunday, those who were commissioned to proclaim the gospel, to make disciples of all nations, continued his proclamation of the kingdom both in their words and in their deeds. In the days after the ascension of Jesus, the apostles proclaimed the good news and healed the sick, drove out demons, and raised the dead.[3] The Word was proclaimed and the sacred meal was shared.[4] Those who heard the good news proclaimed repented and were baptized in the name of Jesus Christ.[5] What Jesus had done himself during his public ministry, his disciples were now performing in his name. During the final supper before his death, Jesus spoke about the works his followers would do after he was gone. "Amen, amen, I say to you, whoever believes in me will do the works that I do, and will do greater ones than these, because I am going to the Father."[6] The early church believed its mission was to do the works Jesus had done, to proclaim the kingdom in word and deed as Jesus himself had done while he was with them.

For the church through the ages, its mission found clear articulation in the final commission given to the disciples on that hilltop in Galilee portrayed in the Gospel of Matthew. "Go, therefore, and make disciples of all nations, baptizing them in the name of the Father, and of the Son, and of the holy Spirit, teaching them to observe all that I have commanded you."[7] Just as Jesus healed, forgave, and called, so too has the church through the centuries continued to heal, forgive, and call in his name. It is this recognition that rests at the foundation of the church's identity and mission, that the church is called to continue doing the kinds of things Jesus did and standing for the values for which Jesus stood. To celebrate the sacraments in the Catholic Church is to continue the mission of Jesus in each subsequent age. The Baltimore Catechism's definition of a sacrament, memorized by generations of Catholic schoolchildren, affirmed that a sacrament is 'a visible sign of an invisible grace.' Affirmed by the newest Catholic Cat-

---

3. Acts 3:1-10; 5:12-16; 20:7-12.
4. Acts 6:2; 1 Cor. 11:23-26.
5. Acts 2:37-42.
6. John 14:12.
7. Matt. 28:19-20.

echism promulgated during the pontificate of John Paul II,[8] these signs are instituted by Christ and entrusted to the church for the purpose of dispensing to the faithful the blessing of divine life. Sacraments are outward signs instituted by Christ to give grace. Sacraments, therefore, have their origin in the words and deeds of Jesus during his earthly ministry and continue in the life and pastoral ministry of the church.

In the Roman Catholic tradition, there are seven such signs or sacraments. They are: Baptism, Confirmation, Eucharist, Reconciliation, Anointing of the Sick, Matrimony, and Holy Orders. A popular classification of the sacraments further divides them along the lines of the goal each sacrament pursues. Baptism, Confirmation, and Eucharist are often referred to as sacraments of initiation because they are the sacraments, celebrated over time by most believers, that initiate one into the Catholic community. Reconciliation and Anointing of the Sick are categorized as sacraments of healing. And Matrimony and Holy Orders are sacraments of vocation for they represent two of the basic vocations to which God calls his people and through which the faithful live their gospel summons to holiness. Together, these sacraments are instruments of God's grace to the believer and believing community throughout the course of the individual's and church's life. In response to the first part of the question that gives this chapter its title, the sacraments are the seven normative sacramental actions through which the church continues the mission of Jesus in its own life and work.

Lowercase Sacraments

Before addressing each of the seven sacraments and what they do, I would like to offer a brief reflection regarding a broader conception of sacraments in the church. As mentioned in my answer to the question regarding scripture, the Catholic tradition is fond of making distinctions between upper and lowercase theological realities. For example, there is the Tradition and tradition of the church. So, too, we can make a similar distinction among the sacraments. Technically, sacraments in the church refer to the seven sacraments identified above. These are the uppercase 'S' Sacraments. But, more broadly, the church also acknowledges the existence of lowercase sacraments. Generally speaking, a lowercase sacrament is any person, thing, event, place, etc. that reveals the presence of God. For some, a mountain vista, a beautiful sunrise, or a lovely sunset might affirm the reality and

8. *Catechism of the Catholic Church*, 1113-1130.

presence of God. For others, it might be an act of unexpected kindness. For still others, it might be a work of art, be it fiction, film, painting, or poem. Perhaps an event, like the birth of a child, marriage to one's beloved, or the death of a parent might inspire an experience of God's presence and love. Each of these places, images, people, or events can open a person to the existence of God. As such, they are lowercase sacraments for their ability to open the human heart to God's presence.

But, there is also a moral call embedded in the recognition of such lowercase sacraments. The old adage that our lives might be the only bible some people will ever read speaks to our intrinsic call as believers to be sacraments in the world. Fundamental to the call of every Christian is the challenge to be the presence of Christ in the lives of those we encounter each day whether we encounter them in our own homes, on the street, in our workplaces, driving our cars, or while shopping at the grocery store. Understood this way, the call of each Christian is to be a sacrament in the world, to respond to God's call to reveal Christ to others. Though not the official sacramental actions of the believing community, our call to be lowercase sacraments represents each believer's response to the fundamental call of Jesus to follow in his footsteps by doing the kinds of things he would do, saying the kinds of things he would say, representing the kinds of values for which he lived and died, and being the kind of person he was and is. Each of us in our own way and in our own little corner of the world, can continue the mission of Jesus by committing ourselves to be lowercase sacraments, revealing in and through our lives the presence of the God who loves us and calls each of us to discipleship.

The Seven Sacraments and What They Do

Having identified the seven Sacraments celebrated by the Roman Catholic Church, the second part of the question in this chapter's title concerns what these seven sacraments do. Though each of the sacraments represents a source of God's grace, each sacrament is also distinct in the blessing poured out on the believers celebrating that particular sacrament. God's love finds distinctive forms of expression depending upon the sacrament being celebrated. Sacraments are not unlike love in this regard. The type of love offered depends upon the broader relationship involved. For instance, we can offer love to our spouse, to our children, to our neighbor, to the poor, or to victims of a natural disaster. Each circumstance or relationship requires a different form or expression of love. The love uniting me with my spouse is very different than the love shared with a neighbor or a victim of a natural disaster. In the same way, each sacrament offers us an experience of God's love in a different form or expression.

Sacraments of Initiation

As mentioned above, the sacraments of Baptism, Confirmation, and Eucharist are sometimes grouped together under the umbrella title of Sacraments of Initiation. These sacraments establish the foundation for Christian life and the celebration of the other sacraments. These sacraments also mirror the course of natural life. Through baptism, we are born anew into a life that is strengthened through the sacrament of Confirmation and is nourished throughout the span of one's years through the celebration of the Eucharist. Through the celebration of these three sacraments the believer is gradually initiated both into the life of Christ and into the life of the church. They provide the foundation and the ongoing nourishment necessary for participation in divine life and for our growth in love. But, as discussed above concerning unique forms and expressions of love, each of these sacraments contributes something unique to the process of initiation into the life of Christ, the life of the church, and the life of faith.

Baptism

As portrayed in the bible, in the aftermath of the departure of the Hebrew slaves from Egypt, the Pharaoh regretted allowing the slaves to leave. Having experienced a change of heart, he led his army, his chariots and horsemen, into the desert chasing after the Hebrew people. Catching up to the former slaves now pinned against the sea, the presence of the powerful Egyptian Army encourages some of the Hebrew people to complain bitterly to Moses, suggesting that he had led them from the safety and security of Egypt to die at the end of the sword in the wilderness. But, Moses assured them that God would fight for them and they would witness God's victory over the Egyptian army. The final editor of the Book of Exodus has blended differing accounts into one narrative that combines distinct versions of the event, one in which the wheels of Pharaoh's chariots get clogged in mud and the other, and far more popular, version indicating that God held the sea to the right and left so the Hebrews might pass through safely, allowing the

Part III: Sacraments

water to return and covering the Egyptians and destroying Pharaoh's army. Regardless of the answer to the question of how the Hebrews escaped, what the ancient Jews recalled in this story was that God saved them, however God saved them, leading them through the water to the joy of new life and the promise of a new homeland.[9]

For early Christians, they saw the story of God's saving action at the sea as a foreshadowing of the gift of baptism through which the believer entered into new life by passing through the water. In the Book of Genesis, it was the spirit hovering over the waters of creation through which God brought forth the cosmos in the first creation story.[10] Later, Noah, his family, and the members of the animal kingdom he shepherded onto his ark, became the progenitors of a new creation in the aftermath of the flood.[11] Like the Hebrew slaves later in the biblical narrative, Noah and his family passed through the water to the far shore of new life. Water was, and remains a rich and necessary ingredient for life. As such, it has always possessed tremendous symbolic power, symbolizing the blessing of life. But, the power of water also evokes death. It was through water that God destroyed the earth, a destruction from which Noah is spared. The water that parts to spare the Hebrew slaves rains death and destruction down upon the Egyptian army. For Christianity, the rich symbol of water would call to mind both its life-giving capacity and its death-dealing power. The waters of baptism have served as the entrance to new and eternal life since the earliest days of the church, a significant step on our pilgrimage to being with God forever. But, water's destructive potential also represents the complex image of the cross, bringing life through an instrument of death, the death the person passes through symbolically in the waters of baptism.

The term baptism comes from the Greek word baptizein which means to immerse or plunge. For Christian faith, the immersion in the water represents the person's burial with Christ in death only to rise from the water to share in Christ's resurrection as a new creation. Thus, the person to be baptized, the catechumen, is baptized not only into the life of Christ and the life of the church but into the very structure of human existence, a structure shaped by the realities of death and life. For Christianity, the reality and finality of death establishes a fundamental limit to human existence. As the French-born Quaker minister Stephen Grellet rightly suggests, we shall

---

9. Exodus 14:1-31.
10. Genesis 1:1-2.
11. Genesis 6:5-9:17.

not pass this way again. This fundamental limit to human life creates the foundational framework within which human beings live out their days. The finality of death affirms the importance of the decisions we make along the way because we cannot stop the relentless unfolding of time. No matter how much we may want to make time stop or at least slow down, we know we cannot. The parents' new baby seems in a blink to be heading to college. The deliriously happy couple on their wedding day soon finds themselves celebrating their 25th wedding anniversary. The life that seemed so long in anticipation when our only desire was to grow up now looks so short in retrospect when we find ourselves trying desperately to hold on.

The specter of death casts its shadow over us throughout the course of our lives, not simply at the end of it. Whereas it is true that we die a physical death but once, we die countless times throughout our lives. The end of a cherished relationship, the loss of a job, the death of a loved one, or the death of a dream might all be instances when we experience a foreshadowing of the ultimate death awaiting us. But, if death casts its dark shadow over our lives so too does the light of new life. The person suffering from the end of a relationship soon meets someone new. The loss of a job might open us to a new and more rewarding career path. The loss of a loved one might increase our appreciation for them, our gratitude for them, and a new experience of their presence in our lives. Saying goodbye to a long-held dream might inspire us to develop a new and more exciting dream. It is true that we experience death often in our lives. But, it is also true that we experience the gift of new life. As our experiences of death unite us to Jesus' crucifixion, so too do our experiences of new life unite us to his resurrection. In baptism, we are buried with Christ in the hope that we too shall rise with him, not only at the end of our days but throughout them.

What the sacrament of Baptism accomplishes can be seen clearly in the signs and symbols at work in the sacramental celebration. The person to be baptized is marked with the sign of the cross signifying both that the person is now marked with the sign of the one to whom the newly baptized will belong, Christ, and of the saving significance of his cross. The Word of God, the foundational narrative of the community, is proclaimed, the Word which reveals the presence of the One calling the person to be baptized to the water, to the life of faith, to the believing community, and to relationship with the Blessed Trinity. The one to be baptized renounces Satan, renounces the evil which Satan seeks to inspire, and to reject Satan by turning more powerfully to God. The person is then immersed in holy water three times or has holy water poured on their forehead three times, signifying their immersion in the life of the Trinity. The water is both a sign of life and a ritual washing away of original sin. The one being baptized is then anointed with oil that has been consecrated by the bishop representing the gift of the Holy Spirit received by the newly baptized. A white garment is placed upon the newly baptized expressing the person's having now put on new life in Christ as well as communicating the innocence of new life in Christ. A candle lighted from the paschal candle, symbolic of Christ's death and resurrection, is presented to the newly baptized, proclaiming that the person has been enlightened by Christ who is the light of the world but also calling the newly baptized to pursue the mission of all disciples to be the salt of the earth and the light of the world.[12]

Having been baptized, the person has received forgiveness of sins, is now a new creation in Christ, is incorporated into the life of the church, incorporates the newly baptized into the sacramental bond that unites all Christians, and receives an indelible spiritual mark. Perhaps the most important quest in the life of the believer is not discovering who we are but whose we are. Baptism marks us as belonging to Christ, making of us a new person shaped by the life, death, and resurrection of Jesus and inspired and guided by the Holy Spirit to follow the Lord's call to take up our cross daily and follow him. Through baptism, we enter through the gateway of faith, not in the belief that the sacrament ends our journey but rather proclaiming its beginning. Through the gift of faith received through the grace of the sacrament, the baptized are called to grow in faith and love, revealing in their lives the presence and love of the God who calls us into being and guides us to enter more deeply into and reflect more powerfully the mystery of Christ's death and resurrection throughout our life.

Confirmation

The Gospel of Luke proclaims that it was through the Holy Spirit that Mary conceived and bore Jesus.[13] It is the Spirit who descends upon Jesus at his baptism then leads him into the desert to be tempted by the devil.[14] It is the same Spirit who anoints Jesus to engage in his ministry of announcing the

---

12. Matt. 5:13-16.
13. Luke 1:35.
14. Luke 3:21-22; 4:1-2.

Kingdom of God in both word and deed.[15] But, the Holy Spirit is not solely present to Jesus alone. The Spirit is also present in and to those to whom Jesus promises the Spirit. When his followers are dragged before synagogues and rulers, the believer is not to worry about what they are to say. It will be the Holy Spirit who will teach them what they are to say.[16] It is the risen Jesus who commissions the disciples to proclaim in his name the forgiveness of sins to all nations beginning in Jerusalem.[17] But, Jesus instructed them to wait in the city until they received the promised power from on high, the gift of the Holy Spirit.[18] On Pentecost, the Spirit descended upon the apostles as tongues of flame. Filled with the Holy Spirit, they began to fulfill their call from Jesus to proclaim the gospel to the ends of the earth.[19] It is the Holy Spirit that has been inspiring and guiding the life and mission of the church and of individual believers since the very beginning.

Initially, confirmation was celebrated at the same time as baptism. Those preparing for initiation into the church could experience long periods of preparation for initiation, culminating with the celebration of the sacraments of initiation at the Easter Vigil. Given that the proper minister of the sacraments was the bishop, the bishop celebrated the sacraments of initiation with those communities under his pastoral care and authority. However, as the church began to grow in numbers and spread throughout the known world, over time the sacraments of initiation were separated. The bishop could not personally attend the Easter celebrations of each community, far too numerous were they to allow for the bishop's presence. Confirmation became separated from baptism and was celebrated whenever the bishop could be present. To this day, most Roman Catholics celebrate the sacrament of Confirmation at a time well beyond the celebration of their Baptism. However, for adults seeking initiation into the Catholic Church, The Rite of Christian Initiation of Adults (RCIA) was established and reconnects the celebration of the sacraments of initiation at the Easter Vigil. For these reasons, the order of the sacraments may be different for different believers pursuing initiation at different moments in their life.

The Sacrament of Confirmation serves as the completion of baptismal grace. When the sacrament is celebrated at a later time, the celebration

15. Luke 4:18-21.
16. Luke 12:12.
17. Luke 24:46-47.
18. Luke 24:49.
19. Acts 1:8.

includes the renewal of baptismal promises as an indication of the necessary interconnectedness of these two sacraments of the church. The confirmed believers enter more deeply into the bond of unity with the church and enter more deeply into relationship with the Holy Spirit living within them. Resulting from the depth of the bond created by the celebration of the sacrament, confirmed believers bear a greater responsibility to proclaim in word and deed the good news of what God has done for us in Jesus through the Spirit. Through the laying on of hands, the apostles conferred on new believers the gift of the Holy Spirit, a gift promised by Jesus.[20] Through the anointing of the confirmed believer, the person is permanently marked with the seal of Christ. This permanent seal marks our "complete belonging to Christ, our enrollment in his service forever,"[21] and the promise that he will be with us always.

The primary effect of the sacrament of Confirmation is the special outpouring of the Holy Spirit experienced by the apostles on that first Pentecost. The sacrament roots us more deeply in the life of the family of God, recognizing Jesus as our brother with whom we call out to God as Father. Confirmation unites us more firmly to Christ, increases the gifts of the Holy Spirit, reinforces our bond with the church, and strengthens us to fulfill our call to proclaim in word and deed our faith in Christ.[22] In the Franco Zeffirelli film "Jesus of Nazareth," there is a scene in which Peter speaks with Matthew about the promise he made to his wife to return home after spending some time with Jesus. Matthew encourages Peter not to lie to himself or his wife, suggesting that their lives, and the lives of every person in the world, will never be the same. And they were among the first to know why. Through the grace of the sacraments and our maturing faith, we too are among those who know why the lives of everyone in the whole world will never be the same. Like the apostles, the first and unique witnesses of the risen Jesus, we too are witnesses of, from, and to the risen Jesus and his significance for the meaning and purpose of human life. Strengthened by the gift of the Holy Spirit, we are called through our celebration of the sacrament of Confirmation to witness to our life and history-shaping faith.

Like baptism, confirmation is also only celebrated once since in and through it we are marked with the special seal of Christ. In a culture and society that places so much emphasis, and often rightly so, on freedom

---

20. John 14:15-17.
21. *Catechism of the Catholic Church*, 1296.
22. Ibid., 1303.

and independence, the sacrament of Confirmation presents us with the challenging reality that we are not independent, that our lives are not our own. The deepest identity we possess is that we belong to Christ. The term messiah is the Jewish equivalent of the Greek term Christos. Both terms mean anointed. In ancient Judaism, the kings of Israel were anointed kings by God. The Jewish belief in a coming messiah expressed their belief in a future king, anointed by God to proclaim the fulfillment of God's promises. Jesus was God's anointed, God's messiah, the Christ. To be anointed with the sacred chrism in the sacrament of Confirmation is to sealed with the sign of Christ, to become a Christ, an anointed, for the world. To be confirmed is to be marked with the sign of Jesus the Christ and commit our lives to being Christ for others.

Eucharist

Despite the use of the somewhat misleading identifying terms of liberal and conservative in American politics, all Americans in our system of government are liberal. What matters is what kind of liberal we are. There have been two primary forms of liberalism in the history of the United States, humanistic liberalism and reform liberalism.[23] Humanistic liberalism, which looks to Thomas Jefferson as its intellectual godfather, emphasizes the freedom of the individual in the formation and attainment of individual goals. A principle thrust of Jeffersonian liberalism is its assertions about the reality of negative freedom. Negative freedom refers to the absence of restraint or what is sometimes called "freedom from." In the context of the United States, humanistic liberalism envisions freedom from taxes, government intrusion, imposed limitations, and governmental coercion. When examined theologically, humanistic liberalism suggests a freedom from our own worst impulses, freedom from sin, from death, from fear, or from despair.

Reform liberalism, which looks to John Adams as its intellectual godfather, rejected the moral neutrality of humanistic liberalism. For the humanists, individuals were free from government or other forms of intervention that they might pursue and attain their own personal goals. Rejecting such neutrality, the reform liberals argued in favor of policies that would encourage and enable human beings to develop their faculties to the highest possible state. In other words, the state was not neutral in what goals to pursue. And its policies should be developed in such a way as to

---

23. See McPherson, *Drawn with the Sword*, p.183ff.

encourage the creation of good, contributing citizens. The reform liberals did not necessarily object to freedom from but insisted that freedom from was intended for a higher expression of freedom, "freedom for." Theologically speaking, if we are free from ourselves, sin, death, fear, and despair, we are so that we might more actively express our freedom in the pursuit of life, fulfillment, happiness, hope, and love. Freedom from imposition and coercion makes us free for goodness, mercy, and love.

The experience of the ancient Hebrews enslaved in Egypt involved both types of freedoms. On the surface, through the leadership of Moses they were being freed from slavery, from the yoke of oppression in Egypt. But, through their liberation from slavery they were being freed for a new life as God's holy people. The final plague, the slaughter of the firstborn of every household in Egypt,[24] tipped the scale in favor of the Hebrews and encouraged the Pharaoh to free the slaves. The Hebrews were protected from the terrible consequence of this final plague, having received directions through Moses to smear lamb's blood on the doorposts and lintel of the homes in which they would eat the meal Moses instructed them to eat.[25] The horrible devastation wrought by this final plague convinced Pharaoh to free the Hebrew slaves. Thus, the people were free from slavery in Egypt.

But, freedom from slavery was only the beginning of the journey that would eventually lead them to the land flowing with milk and honey, the land promised them through Abraham so long ago.[26] The Hebrew people were not free just to be free. They were free from bondage that they might enter into the freedom of new life. The Passover meal was the great celebration, the great memorial, of God's liberating power expressed on behalf of an enslaved people. This meal that all succeeding generations of believers were instructed to eat was to be celebrated annually as a perpetual institution, celebrating God's liberation of the people from slavery to the life of freedom. The covenant God made with Abraham had established the fundamental identity and mission of the people of Israel. But, it was the Passover-Exodus event that would offer the definitive interpretation of that event. It would become the lens through which Israel's subsequent religious and historical experience would be interpreted and understood. The Passover-Exodus would become the defining moment for a people often subjugated by foreign powers, who often found themselves hoping for freedom

24. Exodus 12:29-32.
25. Exodus 12:1-28.
26. Genesis 15:1-21.

from oppression, and who continually longed for spiritual liberation that they might live as children of God. It was this transition from freedom from to freedom for that found expression in the perpetual institution of the Passover meal. And it was on the night before he died that Jesus redefined the Passover meal, a meal and a death through which we would be freed from death to the freedom of life.

In the Dogmatic Constitution of the Church, Lumen Gentium, the Fathers of the Second Vatican Council proclaimed the Eucharist to be the source and summit of Catholic life.[27] The Eucharist completes the believer's initiation into the life of God and the church begun at baptism. The Eucharist, a word that means 'thanksgiving,' is the means by and through which the whole church offers its thanks to God for the blessings bestowed upon it through Christ in the Holy Spirit. It is also an opportunity for the church to give itself to God just as Christ gave himself to the church through the sacrament. On the night before he died, when at supper with his closest friends, he transformed the liberation from slavery to freedom celebrated in the Passover meal into a celebration of the liberation from death to life to be effected by his death and resurrection. The bread of Passover became his body to be broken, taken, and eaten by his followers. The cup of wine became his blood, blood poured out for the many for the forgiveness of sins. The meal became a memorial and sacrament of his death offered for the life of all, a life foreshadowed in his resurrection.

In that gift of self, the gift of his own life memorialized in the Eucharist, the church proclaims it is the real presence of Christ himself we receive in the Eucharist. On the night of his betrayal, Jesus was confronting the very real dilemma that he had to face his destiny, that he had to leave, yet wanted to stay. To solve this dilemma, Jesus crafted the perfect gift through which he could leave and yet remain, that he could suffer death on the cross and yet truly remain present with and to his people forever. The gift he devised that would allow for his genuine and continuing presence was the gift of the Eucharist, a truth given expression in the church's teaching of transubstantiation.[28] The Catholic Church maintains that the whole substance of the bread and wine are changed into the whole substance of the body and blood of Christ. The body and blood, the soul and divinity of Christ are truly, really, and substantially contained under the Eucharistic

---

27. Lumen Gentium, 11.

28. This way of understanding the institution of the Eucharist I owe to a homily by the great Jesuit preacher Walter Burghardt.

Part III: Sacraments

species of bread and wine.[29] By this the church means that the essence of the bread and wine are transformed through the power and presence of the Holy Spirit in the church's prayer of consecration. Though retaining all of the physical elements of bread and wine, at the level of essence, they are no longer bread and wine but the body and blood of Christ. As a child, I remember my dad taking me to see the movie "The Exorcist." During the movie, a priest informs the mother, who believes her daughter to be possessed, that he sprinkled holy water on her and the girl reacted very violently. He tells the mother it was tap water, a distinction the import of which evades the mother. The priest clarifies that holy water is blessed. In that scene, the viewer is introduced into a penetrating Catholic truth. On the surface, the water still looks, tastes, and behaves like water. But, at a deeper level it is no longer water because it has been blessed and, though unobserved and unprovable, the water is now at the level of its essence holy water. When two people in love stand before the right people and proclaim the right words, they become spouses in the eyes of God and the larger human community. They look the same, speak the same, and walk the same but now they are married, one in love. In the same way, the Eucharistic species of bread and wine may still look, taste, and behave like bread and wine. But, at a deeper level they have been transformed into the body and blood of Christ. And, for as long as the church exists, we will continue to gather around the altar to receive the body and blood of Christ, to continue to gather in memory of him who died and rose for us, and to commit ourselves as individual believers and as a community of faith to being shaped by the Eucharist, to become a people willing to give our body and blood for love of others.

Some communities only offer the Eucharistic bread, or body of Christ, to the gathered assembly. The question is, therefore, often asked about whether receiving only the body of Christ is sufficient to receive communion. Wrestled with at the Council of Trent, the council fathers decreed that Christ was truly present, whole and entire, in each of the species and whole and entire in each of the parts.[30] Therefore, to receive either the body or the blood of Christ is to receive Christ whole and entire. Though it is obviously preferred wherever and whenever possible to receive communion under both forms, it is nevertheless true that the reception of communion under one form does not represent any diminishment of the reception of Christ by the believing

---

29. Catechism of the Catholic Church, 1374.
30. Catechism of the Catholic Church, 1377.

community. In both forms, once the bread and wine have been transformed into the body and blood of Christ at the level of essence, the species remain the body and blood of Christ for as long as the species exists.[31]

In sum, the Eucharist is the meeting point between the life and ministry of the church and the God who, through Jesus, reconciled himself to the world. Through the Eucharist, an unbloodied celebration of the once for all sacrifice of the cross, Christ continues his work of redemption. But, it is also through the Eucharist that the church, the people of God, respond to the gifts and promises of God with praise, adoration, and a commitment to share in the paschal mystery of Christ's life, death, and resurrection into which each believer was baptized. The Eucharist is also an anticipation of the heavenly banquet when all of God's promises will at last be fulfilled, when God presides over the marriage of the new heaven and new earth when God will be all in all. In the Eucharist, the believing community remembers the past actions of God through Christ in the Spirit, commits to a Eucharistic life of self-giving love within the bonds of the believing community's mission to make disciples of all nations through love of God and neighbor, and anticipates the future when the reign of God proclaimed and embodied in the life of Jesus will at last be fully realized.

Sacraments of Healing

It is evident from the gospel tradition that Jesus engaged in acts of healing. Through the power of Jesus' human and divine love, the blind regained their sight, lepers were made clean, the lame could walk, and the dead were restored to life. These healings were not physical cures alone. Illness not only had a somatic consequence but also resulted in separation from the community. Jesus' healings not only restored the person to health but perhaps more importantly, restored the person's relationship to and with the community. Lepers were an exiled people,[32] the woman with the hemorrhage was defiled by the flow of blood making impossible her participation in the religious life of the community,[33] the priest and Levite in Jesus' parable of the Good Samaritan pass by the wounded traveler on the side of the

---

31. For this reason, the body of Christ is housed in a tabernacle rather than somewhere else as testament to the fact that once it is transformed, it remains so.
32. Mark 1:40-45.
33. Matt. 9:20-22.

road for fear that they would become ritually impure,[34] and the paralytic pondered whether his affliction was the result of the sin of his parents or his own, sins that cut him off from the life of the community.[35] Illness had a social consequence, alienating and isolating the weak, removing them from the life and/or presence of the community.

For Jesus to heal the physical ailment not only brought physical relief but also reunion. If their illness, perceived by many as the result of God's punishment for sin, removed them from the community, their healing restored them to life in that community. It was not simply that the lame could now walk, the blind could now see, the leper was now clean, or the dead person was now alive, as if that would not have been enough. No longer were they shunned by their own community. Rather, they were invited back into the life of the community, allowed once again to participate in its rituals and customs. These acts also revealed God to be on the side of those who suffer. They represented a statement about the inbreaking of the kingdom of God and its victory over those forces to which the people of Jesus' time believed they were susceptible: death, illness, demons, and nature. Jesus' healings proclaimed that the powers opposed to God's love were on the path to being defeated at last, a victory of goodness over sin and evil that was ushering in the long-awaited reign of God.

But, the healing of forgiveness was also, and in the minds of some, the critical dimension of the gift of God offered through the life and ministry of Jesus. The Gospel of Matthew, in its portrayal of the Last Supper, emphasizes the importance of forgiveness, identifying it as the primary result of the death Jesus was to die on the cross the next day. "Drink from it, all of you; for this is my blood of the covenant, which is poured out for many for the forgiveness of sins."[36] Earlier in Matthew's gospel, Jesus instructs Peter that there should be no limit to the believer's willingness to forgive.[37] Forgiveness is a particular theme in the Gospel of Luke, demonstrated by Jesus himself through his willingness to forgive his executioners while hanging on the cross and his offer of reconciliation to the repentant thief.[38] It is Jesus' persistent willingness to offer God's forgiveness that has provided some of the most memorable moments in his ministry. In the process of extending

34. Luke 10:25-37.
35. Luke 5:17-26.
36. Mat. 26:27-28.
37. Matt. 18:21-22.
38. Luke 23:34, 39-43.

mercy to the woman caught in the act of adultery, Jesus tells those standing by who were all too willing to judge and condemn that "anyone among you who is without sin be the first to throw a stone at her."[39] When a woman of ill repute approaches Jesus while reclining at table with some Pharisees, he instructs the Pharisees that her sins are forgiven her because of the greatness of her love.[40] If sin is what separates us from God, forgiveness is the primary vehicle through which our relationship with God is renewed. It is for the purpose of restoring and developing this relationship that God chose to become one of us and why forgiveness and reconciliation were so central to Jesus' life and ministry.

Jesus continues to reach out to heal the sick and the lame, the blind and the dying. When he sent the Twelve out on mission, Jesus included in his instructions to them that they were to cure the sick, raise the dead, cleanse the lepers, and cast out demons.[41] To the apostles, he entrusted the ministry of healing, a ministry they pursued both before Jesus' death and after.[42] Although popularly this sacrament continues to be referred to as Last Rites, Anointing of the Sick is a sacrament celebrated with and for those who are gravely ill and, in the event that a person experiences grave illness more than once in a lifetime, is a repeatable sacrament. For those who celebrate and are about to leave this life, the church offers the believer Viaticum. Viaticum refers to the reception of Holy Communion that provides nourishment for the final journey and the completion of our earthly pilgrimage. By celebrating the Sacrament of the Sick, the person receives the grace of the consolation of the Holy Spirit to strengthen them and bring them peace. In addition, they experience greater union with the suffering of Christ, greater union with the church community whom they strengthen through the example of their faith in the face of suffering, and for those who are departing this life, it prepares them for their final journey back to the God who is both their origin and destiny.

Jesus also continues to offer the redeeming power of forgiveness to all through the sacramental ministry of the church. In the Sacrament of Reconciliation, also popularly known as confession and penance though both words highlight aspects of the sacrament and not its totality, Jesus speaks words of comfort and mercy to the repentant. Though we are washed clean

---

39. John 8:7.
40. Luke 7:36-50.
41. Matt. 10:8.
42. Acts 3:1-10; 5:12-16; 9:34; 14:3.

of sin through baptism, we continue to fall short of the glory to which God calls us. Through selfishness, arrogance, or weakness, we continue to wound the relationship that binds us with God and with one another. Though the spirit is indeed willing, the flesh is weak and time and again we commit sinful acts, fall into sinful patterns of behavior, or intentionally reject the love God offers us. But, we are never beyond the limits of God's compassion and mercy. Jesus affirms for us that there is more rejoicing in heaven over the return of one repentant sinner than for 99 righteous persons with no need for repentance.[43] Of course, lest we suffer from a sinful lack of humility, it is important that we recognize that, in truth, we are throughout our lives the lost sinner whom God seeks out. The depth of God's love brings into sharp focus our need for forgiveness and the importance of repentance. It is no mystery why Jesus began his public ministry by calling people to repentance.[44] One must repent if one is to inherit the kingdom and embody the good news in their own lives.

In my experience, the two most popular questions asked by believers concerning the sacrament of reconciliation are, "Why do I have to go to a priest to be forgiven? Can't I just ask God for forgiveness myself?" Concerning the former, it is important to state at the outset that the priest is not forgiving the believer in the sacrament. The priest administers the sacrament but it is not the priest who forgives. In the words of absolution spoken by the priest, it is God through Jesus who offers to the person forgiveness and the invitation to reconcile. It should be affirmed that this is true in all sacramental celebrations in the church. It is God who baptizes, confirms, consecrates bread and wine, heals, forgives and calls. We are all called as Christians to be the presence of Christ in the world. In the celebration of the sacraments, Christ is present in the person and office of the priest, continuing the ministry he began two thousand years ago in Galilee.

But, why do I have to go to the priest for forgiveness? If God hears my prayers, why can God not grant me forgiveness on my own? Why do I need to go through the priest? Though more could probably be said, three points should be made. First, you can and should maintain an active prayer life and when appropriate repent to God, asking for forgiveness. The sacrament does not prohibit believers from asking God for forgiveness. So, the answer to 'why can't I' is simply 'you can.' Second, the New Testament makes clear that Jesus chose to continue his mission through the ministry

---

43. Luke 15:7.
44. Mark 1:14-15.

of the community he left behind. The Eucharistic meal was not intended to be celebrated by an individual believer at home alone with a loaf of bread and a bottle of Merlot. Continuing the mission of Jesus was and is a necessarily communal experience. One of the challenges contemporary Americans face when reading the biblical testimony concerns the bible's communal vision which stands in sharp contrast to our emphasis on the individual. Not that the individual vanishes in the biblical writings, but it is nevertheless true that the bible places great and primary emphasis on 'we' rather than 'I.' Contemporary believers worry about going to heaven, a problematic statement to begin with, rather than the bible's communal vision of the end time and the fulfillment of God's promises. American culture places such tremendous emphasis on my relationship with God, it often jettisons the equally important emphasis on relationship with God as a communal reality. It is this diminishment of the communal that has given rise to a large segment of the population increasingly defining themselves as spiritual but not religious. They want the relationship with God but not the communal ties the bible saw as necessary for the creation and growth of that relationship.

In addition to this communal emphasis, forgiveness functions in much the same way as illness did in the time of Jesus. As we discussed above, illness alienated the person from the life of the community. In the same way, sin has the power to alienate and isolate us from the community. Forgiveness then not only has the power to heal but also to reconcile one with God and with the community that sin has wounded. Therefore, in the sacrament the priest not only represents Christ who extends forgiveness to the believer but also the community that welcomes the sinner back. Some writers point to the cross as expressing both the vertical dimension of our relationship with God and the horizontal dimension of our relationship to and with each other. The full experience of the life of faith requires both dimensions. In the Sacrament of Reconciliation, the believer asks for and receives forgiveness from God while simultaneously being reconciled with the believing community. All sacraments are necessarily public celebrations, reminding us that the life of faith is never simply about God and me but about God and us.

Part III: Sacraments

The Sacraments of Vocation or Service

Arguably, the two most controversial sacraments are Holy Orders and Matrimony. Holy Orders is the sacrament by and through which men are ordained to service in the church and Matrimony is the sacrament through which two people are united in the grace of marriage. These two are controversial because the first is based upon the assumption that the Last Supper was the first ordination ceremony through which Jesus ordained his apostles the first priests and the second because it is very difficult to trace matrimony back to the life and ministry of Jesus. It is obvious that Jesus healed the sick, forgave sinners, and commanded his followers to share the bread and the wine in memory of him. But, one does not find Jesus presiding at weddings, despite convoluted arguments involving Jesus' miracle at the wedding feast at Cana. Nevertheless, Holy Orders and Matrimony are defined as sacraments in the Roman Catholic tradition. Though perhaps not possessing as clear a connection to Jesus' ministry as other sacraments, it remains true that Orders and Matrimony sacramentalize our call to service in Jesus' name.

The entire church is a priestly people. "... you are a chosen race, a royal priesthood, a holy nation, God's own people, in order that you may proclaim the mighty acts of him who called you out of darkness into his marvelous light."[45] Through baptism, all are baptized into a share in the threefold ministry of Christ as priest, prophet, and king. Unlike the view held by some in the church that the work of the church is pursued by priests alone, the priesthood of the baptized affirms the universal call to holiness and service in which we all participate as members of the one body of Christ. But, in addition, the church has long recognized the call to the ministerial priesthood. The ministerial, or ordained, priesthood represents a call to serve the church in the person of Christ. All the baptized share in the common priesthood but those ordained to the ministerial priesthood are called to serve the baptized. They serve the People of God by teaching, by presiding at worship and the celebration of the sacraments, and through governance.

Why is the sacrament called Holy Orders? In ancient Rome, the word order typically referred to an established governing body. To be ordained was to be incorporated into, or become a member of, a governing body. In the church, there are several orders. For instance, those preparing for initiation into the church are members of the order of catechumens. Through

---

45. 1 Peter 2:9.

matrimony, the two become members of the order of spouses. Through ordination, men are sacramentally incorporated into the order either of bishops, priests, or deacons. Bishop, priest, and deacon represent the three degrees of church leadership and governance. Only the bishop has received the fullness of the sacrament. Those ordained priests and deacons are called to support the ministry of the bishop and to serve as his co-workers. Priests do so either through parish ministry or occupying an office in the leadership structure of the diocese. Deacons occupy important roles in the church's proclamation of the Word, service at the altar, and the work of charity within the church and the larger community.

Like baptism, the sacrament of Holy Orders makes an indelible mark on the person and confers the grace of the Holy Spirit necessary to serve in the priestly ministry. In baptism, this indelible mark identifies the person as belonging to Christ. In Orders, the grace of the sacrament signs the person with an indelible mark that bonds the person to Christ so they may serve as the instrument of Christ in service to the church. Although all the baptized are called to be Christ in the world, those ordained to the ministerial priesthood are called to represent Christ in the leadership and governance of the church's life and mission. That does not mean, of course, that everything a priest says and does results from the outpouring of the Holy Spirit upon them anymore than every statement or act of a baptized person is inspired by the Spirt and is therefore free from error. But, like the baptized person, the grace is present to the individual that they might cooperate with the Spirit in faithfully discharging the duties of their specific office and ministry. And, since it is Christ who acts in and through the ordained minister to advance the cause of salvation, the personal faults and foibles of the priest do not prevent the action of Christ in the sacraments and mission of the church from effecting salvation.

When considered as a sacramental, incarnational church, the ministerial priesthood is central to the identity and mission of the community of faith. If the sacraments represent a crucial dimension of the church's continuation of the ministry of Jesus and the ordinary minister of the sacraments is a member of the ministerial priesthood, then the sacrament of Holy Orders is vital for the life of the church. We shall have reason to discuss this centrality again in chapter five. Nevertheless, the church has long understood that when Jesus commissioned his disciples to make disciples of all nations, that commission finds unique embodiment in the ministerial priesthood. "Jesus said to them again, 'Peace be with you. As the Father has sent me, so I send you."[46] The ministerial priesthood is established by the church to offer service, to pass on to each succeeding generation the substance of the faith we share, and to offer leadership and participate in the governance of the community as it moves through history.

Two popular questions arise whenever the discussion turns to the sacrament of Holy Orders. The first involves the discipline of celibacy and the second concerns the question of the role of women in the church. The practice of celibacy has long been associated with the ministerial priesthood, though it has not always been so. Peter was married. The author of the First Letter of Timothy points out in his discussion of the qualifications of a bishop that the person should be married only once.[47] Nevertheless, the practice of mandatory celibacy has been in place for many centuries and that it is also fair to say that the practice was pursued long before it became an official discipline among clergy in the church in the eleventh century. This discipline is often spoken of as a specific form or expression of love in and for the church. In addition, the practical consequences of the discipline free the ordained minister to love all equally and to be available to the community without obstacle or outside demands, for instance the demands of marriage and family life. As a discipline, the church holds that it remains within the authority of the church to suspend, jettison, or adjust this practice if it deems the Spirit is calling it to such a change. However, despite the expectation among some in the aftermath of the Second Vatican Council that the church would institute such a change, the discipline of mandatory celibacy remains in effect in the western church for ordained clergy, with the exception of permanent deacons who can be married men called to the office of the diaconate.

The second, and far more complicated question, concerns the role of women in the church and their specific exclusion from the sacrament of Orders. This question is far too complex to do it justice in this chapter but I will try to map out the opposing views as succinctly as possible. In his 1988 Apostolic Letter *Mulieris Dignitatem*, On the Dignity and Vocation of Women, Pope John Paul II affirms the church's teaching that Christ called only men to be his apostles and that they alone at the Last Supper received the sacramental charge to 'do this in remembrance of me,' and that they alone received the power to forgive sins on Easter night.[48] Through the im-

---

46. John 20:21.
47. 1 Tim. 3:2.
48. John 20:23.

age of Christ as the bridegroom who gives himself completely to his bride the church, the pope argues that Jesus intended to select only men to the priestly and sacramental service of the church through which the bridegroom, the man, would continue to offer himself completely to the bride, his church. Therefore, in this view, it is completely legitimate for the church to maintain that only men can be ordained as representing the expressed wish and desire of Christ.[49]

Critics suggest this view, what is termed the pre-critical or blueprint view of the origin of the church, rests on the claim that Jesus founded a new religion during his lifetime. Grounded on this assumption, the church teaches that Jesus chose from among his followers twelve apostles, provided special training, and made Peter the head of the church. Jesus intentionally created the institutional structure of the church, identifying offices and ministries that had clearly defined levels of authority. Shortly before his death, Jesus instituted the sacraments of the Eucharist and Holy Orders, leading the apostles to view themselves as priests and bishops of the new religion, a religion in which, per Jesus' instructions, only men could be ordained to lead.[50] However, these critics affirm, there is no evidence in the New Testament to support any of these claims. In fact, had Jesus intentionally acted to found a new religion, some disputes in the early church would simply have never occurred, e.g. the debate over Gentile inclusion and the role of circumcision. The historical-critical approach, in opposition to the pre-critical approach, views Jesus as a teacher who proclaimed in word and deed the kingdom of God, who taught with authority, performed acts of power as embodiments of the kingdom's dawning, and laid the foundations for what was to become the church by calling disciples, commissioning them to preach and heal, and "providing for a continued discipleship in the real and symbolic meal that was the Last Supper."[51] He anticipated his rejection and the inclusion of the Gentiles and that, although there was no single form of organization in the New Testament communities, there was never a community without some form of order and structure. As a result, critics reject the blueprint model that would exclude women from the ministerial priesthood and affirm that the church is called to respond to the call of Christ in every age and that the structures, offices, and orders in the church need not stand in fidelity to a blueprint that never existed. Rather,

49. Pope John Paul II, Mulieris Dignitatem, 26.
50. McBrien, *The Church*, 30.
51. Ibid., 30-31.

the church is called to be faithful to the inspiration of the Holy Spirit that animates and guides the church, its identity, structure, and mission.

Regarding matrimony, though one does not encounter Jesus presiding at wedding ceremonies during his earthly ministry, it is nevertheless true that marriage is a consistent and profound image of the love uniting Christ and the church throughout the New Testament.[52] The Book of Revelation uses the image of marriage to proclaim the fulfillment of God's promises at the end of time.[53] The bond of unity between the two spouses is a concrete, historical reflection of the love uniting Christ and his people. And both relationships, human marriage and the church and Christ, are intended to be life-giving. Not only does the marriage foster growth in love and goodness among the spouses, but their intimacy is ordered to the end of new creation through family and/or service. The love uniting the spouses is the seed from which the life of children and community grows and develops. The life-giving character of the marital bond through children or through service to the broader community reflects the life-giving grace offered through Christ in the Spirit that strengthens believers and calls them to a life of holiness.

It is for this reason that the church takes divorce so seriously. If the human bond is an image, a sacrament, of Christ's bond with the church, then the separation or ending of that bond is treated with utmost seriousness, even from the beginning of the proclamation of the gospel. Mark's gospel proscribes divorce though Matthew's gospel does allow for it in the case of infidelity.[54] Though certainly our knowledge of the myriad causes of divorce and the negative effects on children when parents remain in an unhealthy marriage have softened the community's rigor when it comes to divorce, it remains, however, a very serious issue in the life of the church. This is not intended to be a punitive measure against the spouses but a recognition and affirmation of the power of the sacrament and its meaning for the community of faith. Therefore, the issue continues to be the object of thought in the church as the community ponders the contemporary reality of divorce against the backdrop of marriage's purpose as a reflection or expression of the love Christ has for the church.

Hearkening back to the days of the early community, the spouses and children form the domestic church, the earliest and most important

---

52. Ephesians 5:21-33.
53. Rev. 21:1-5.
54. Mark 10:2-12; Matt. 19:3-12.

experience of the faith, especially for children. Even as individual believers are called to be imitators of Christ, so too are families called to be imitators of the Holy Family. It was within the loving bond of family life that Jesus first experienced the love of God his Father, the rich tradition of which he and his family were a part, and the call to serve the broader community. In like manner, the parents are their children's first teachers of the faith. For this reason, parents must make every effort to grow in their knowledge and experience of the Catholic tradition that they might effectively and faithfully pass it on to the next generation. As well formed adult Catholic Christians, the parents become the source of the child's first experience of the love of God, first learn of the importance of sharing in the life of the community, and first hear the call to serve others in love and compassion. In a time when a life of faith can experience numerous challenges from the world and from the church herself, the domestic church takes on increased importance as a center of living faith and attentiveness to our call to lead Christ-like lives of love and mercy.

One final popular issue should be attended to before we end this lengthy chapter. This issue centers on sexual activity outside of the bonds of marriage. Though seeming antiquated and out of touch with the movement of modern life, the church remains committed to its teaching that the only place for sexual activity is within the bond of marriage. Why? Let me begin with an example. When I began my career teaching theology, I started out at the high school level. Teaching at a co-educational Catholic school, I was often privy to relationships forming and ending, developing and changing among members of the student body. Once, a member of the junior class showed me a ring he had bought for a girl he liked in the sophomore class. That evening, they were going out on their second date. The young girl, I learned later, did not respond well to the gift. Why? I suspect it was because the gift was inappropriate, given the level of their relationship. Gifts should always match the depth of the relationship. This is especially true for the church when it comes to the act of sex. The gift of oneself in the act of sex is total and complete and is only appropriate within a relationship in which the two have promised themselves to each other completely and totally. Though people may still disagree with the church's position, I mention it here for the sake of advancing understanding of that position. Too often, the church has been preoccupied with what we do below the belt and not nearly as interested or as dogmatic about other equally or even more important matters. To his credit, Pope Francis has tried to change the tone of the conversation and alter this preoccupation. He has met with some resistance but a great deal of support. Nevertheless, it is worth remembering why the church teaches about the sanctity of sex within marriage, especially at a time when generations of young people are identified as the hook-up generation. Sex is a powerful experience and should continue to be the subject of serious thought and reflection. And whenever experienced, it must always be an expression of a profound and unifying love, a love that reflects the unifying love of Christ for us all.

Conclusion

As human beings, we live within the framework of space and time. Within that framework, love exists not as a free-floating idea but as an embodied reality experienced through concrete acts that express the truth of that love. As a gift to the church that gathers in memory of him and that strives to realize in ever greater ways the kingdom he proclaimed, Jesus bequeathed to the church certain characteristic actions through which his mission continues in each successive age. These actions are both for and from the church. They are for the church for through them the church comes into being. They are from the church in that the church actualizes its identity and mission through its celebration of them. These actions are the seven official sacraments of the Roman Catholic Church. Through the constant celebration of these seven Sacraments and through our persistent willingness to be sacraments in the world, the church continues to discover its identity and purpose even as Christ's work of salvation finds concrete, historical expression.

Chapter 6

God's Grace Made Visible

Thomas M. Tasselmyer

The Reformed Protestant View

On March 18, 1962, I was baptized at St. Joseph's Monastery in Baltimore, Maryland. That's a conspicuous date because it's a full two weeks after I was born; significantly longer than I would have expected my parents to wait considering the importance of baptism in the Roman Catholic church. The wait, however, was justified; my Godparents, traveling from northeast Pennsylvania, had to allow the most powerful nor'easter of the twentieth century to move through. The storm's high winds and battering waves destroyed beaches, and thousands of homes along the Mid-Atlantic coast (think Superstorm Sandy fifty years earlier!), and produced heavy snow and power outages farther inland where we lived. Travel from northeast Pennsylvania to Baltimore was most likely very difficult for several days after my birth.

I received my first Holy Communion on March 26, 1970, at St. Leo's Church in Fairfax, Virginia. It was Holy Thursday. After church, my family celebrated the occasion with ice cream sundaes at the Howard Johnson's restaurant at Fairfax Circle (I ordered the biggest one they sold: The Big Black Cow); it was a very happy day indeed!

Confirmation for me came on April 25, 1976, also at St. Leo's Church in Fairfax, Virginia. I remember some kidding around within my family prior to the ceremony regarding the possibility that the bishop might call on me, should he decide to grill the candidates with a few questions

Part III: Sacraments

about their faith and the confirmation process. You see, our bishop was a "Thomas" like me, so, surely, he would search for another "Thomas" to call on if he decided to go that route. And, in fact, Bishop Thomas Welsh called on a few of us to talk about our confirmation experience, and I was one of them. He asked me why I chose St. Francis for my confirmation name. That was easy; St. Francis liked animals and so did I. I loved to be outdoors camping and fishing and communing with God's creation so St. Francis, the animal-loving saint, seemed perfect for me.

Interestingly, I have no record of my first confession and receiving the sacrament of penance. But, I do recall various Saturday afternoons quietly, and nervously, waiting in the pews of St. Leo's with my three sisters as we waited and watched for the little light over the confessional door to turn from red to green; the signal it was our turn to enter. If it was taking a long time for the light to change it was natural to wonder what required such a lengthy confession, especially if mom, dad, or one of my sisters was the one in there!

I was married to Laurie Bates on February 9, 1985, at North Ridge Christian Missionary Alliance Church in Raleigh, North Carolina. It was a crisp, sunny afternoon and I was more nervous than I had ever been in my life (and I haven't been that nervous since). Standing in the waiting room before the service began I literally got "cold feet"; they felt as frozen as the winter air outside.

In June 2008, I was ordained as a ruling elder in the Presbyterian Church at Hunt Valley Church in Maryland. I wasn't nervous, like I was on my wedding day, but I felt the weight of the moment. To have other elders lay hands on my shoulders and pray for God to use me in the building up of His church was an experience that I won't forget.

I haven't personally received the anointing of the sick, but I have been part of a group of elders called upon to anoint members of our church who were seriously ill.

So, when you add them all up, I have been fortunate enough to personally experience the solemnity, holiness, and spiritual blessings that accompany the seven rituals that Protestants and Catholics consider when studying the sacraments of the church.

And even though I have a hard time remembering the password to my bank or email accounts, I can still remember at least a few aspects of these various ceremonies, some going back nearly fifty years. Why is that?

Why aren't other important life-moments, such as getting my first driver's license, or cashing my first real paycheck, not as solidly etched in my mind?

For me, it helps that my very faithful and devoted Catholic mother made sure that when I left home after college to start my career, I had in my possession, filed safely away, the official documents proving I had received these sacraments. They were probably the only semi-important documents I owned as a 22-year-old, and I still have the paper certificates that mom gave me on the desk in front of me as I write this. But, I believe the real reason that I can remember receiving these sacraments and participating in these spiritual ceremonies is that they were not empty rituals. God has assigned deep spiritual significance to the sacraments. As my faith in Christ has deepened over the years, the Holy Spirit has made the power of the sacraments real and even more memorable.

In Reformed theology, however, those spiritual moments that are lodged in my memory consist of not seven, but two sacraments: baptism and communion. The others: penance, confirmation, marriage, ordination, and anointing the sick, might be considered sacramental, i.e., a visible reminder of God's promises, or simply an important spiritual ceremony, but in Reformed theology they are not considered to be sacraments. Which, of course, begs the question; "Why not?" And that's what this chapter is all about.

Sacrament Defined

There's a good chance that the word "sacrament", as it is used in the church today, comes to us from the work of Tertullian (b. ca. 155), the north African church father who wrote prolifically in Latin during the early part of the third century. In his attempts to bridge the ideological gap between the newness of Christianity and the old paganism of his day, Tertullian coined a great number of new words. For example, he was the first writer to use the term "Trinity" to express the idea of three Persons (Father, Son, and Holy Spirit) in one Godhead. And it seems that Tertullian took the Latin term *sacramentum*, used to translate the Greek *mysterion* meaning "once hidden but now revealed," to refer to the mystery of God's salvific work through Christ, as well as, to the thing that reveals a mystery, such as a symbol or ritual. He was also aware of the sacred oath, or *sacramentum*, that Roman soldiers were required to swear. For the persecuted church in north Africa, a *sacramentum* was how Christians could express solidarity and devotion to Christ, just as soldiers swore allegiance and devotion to Rome.

Part III: Sacraments

Augustine (354-430), the Bishop of Hippo in north Africa in the late fourth and early fifth centuries, moved the theology of sacraments forward by emphasizing the need to have something to see for the mystery to be revealed. For Augustine, a sacrament is a visible form of God's invisible grace. He taught that a sign of a sacred thing is a sacrament, if the sign is in some way related to the thing it is revealing. This very broad definition, however, led him to conclude that even the words in the Creed and the Lord's Prayer were sacred signs of the things they refer to, and so he considered the Creed and the Lord's Prayer sacraments.

By the twelfth century, the theologian Hugh of St. Victor (1096-1141) further refined Augustine's theology by establishing four principles to define a sacrament: 1) there must be a physical element, such as bread, wine, water, oil, etc.; 2) the physical element or sign must, in some way, be like the thing it signifies, such as wine is like blood; 3) there must be an authorization for the sign to signify the spiritual reality, e.g., words of institution from Christ; 4) the power of the sacrament must have an effect on those who receive it. By Hugh's definition, penance could not be a sacrament because there is no physical element associated with it. The incarnation, death, and the church itself, however, were sacraments according to Hugh. Something still was not quite right.

Peter Lombard (c. 1100-1160), Archbishop of Paris in the middle of the twelfth century, removed the requirement of a physical element from Hugh's definition and thereby brought it into alignment with what, in his day, were the widely recognized seven sacraments of the church: baptism, the eucharist (also called communion or the Lord's Supper), confirmation, penance, marriage, ordination, and extreme unction (also called anointing of the sick). Lombard's definition of a sacrament was included in his influential theological book *The Four Books of the Sentences* and it became accepted as the Catholic standard.

However, when the German monk, priest, and theologian named Martin Luther (1483-1546), began to protest corruption in the church in the sixteenth century, one of his primary concerns was the sacramental system, especially the sacrament of penance. In fact, the 95 Theses—points of dispute—that Luther nailed to the door of the Castle Church in Wittenburg, Germany on October 31, 1517, started by questioning this sacrament.

> Thesis #1: When our Lord and Master Jesus Christ said "Repent," he intended that the entire life of believers should be repentance.

> Thesis #2: This word repentance cannot be understood to mean the sacrament of penance, or the act of confession and satisfaction administered by the priests.

Of particular concern to Luther was the idea of the church offering indulgences whereby a penitent sinner, for a price, could be exempt from his acts of penance, or even lessen his own suffering in purgatory, or the suffering of a loved one already deceased.

> Thesis #21: Therefore, those preachers of indulgences are in error, who say that by the pope's indulgences a man is freed from every penalty and is saved.

> Thesis #27: They preach man-made doctrines who say that so soon as the coin jingles into the money-box, the soul flies out of purgatory.

> Thesis #28: It is certain that when the coin jingles into the money-box, greed and avarice can be increased, but the result of the intercession of the church is in the power of God alone.

Luther also questioned the validity of what the church called the "treasury of merit"; an accumulation of extra merit earned by Jesus's sacrifice on the cross and the exemplary lives of the saints, from which the pope doled out indulgences.

> Thesis #56: The treasures of the church, out of which the pope grants indulgences, are not sufficiently named or known among the people of Christ.

> Thesis #62: The true treasure of the church is the most holy gospel of the glory and grace of God.

And he pointedly wondered why, if the pope had the power to alleviate the suffering of the faithful in purgatory, he did not simply give everyone a plenary indulgence, for free:

> Thesis #82: Why does the pope not empty purgatory, for the sake of holy love and for the sake of desperate souls that are there, if he redeems an infinite number of souls for the sake of miserable money with which to build a church? The former reasons would be most just, while the latter is most trivial.

The practice of selling indulgences solidified for Luther the need for the church to reform. In his mind, penance, and the sacraments in general, had become a man-made system of rules and regulations disconnected from the Word of God. The faithful were trying to merit God's favor by participating in the sacramental system, and the pope was using the sacraments as political and economic tools. Luther believed the church needed a reformation centered around two core principles: salvation is by faith alone, not a system of sacraments mediated by priests, bishops, or the pope; and Scripture alone is the source of truth regarding Christian faith and practice, including the sacraments, which cannot be detached from the Word of God, written, and preached.

In 1520, Luther published *The Babylonian Captivity of the Church*, a Latin booklet that harshly criticized the Catholic view of the sacraments and established his own understanding of them. Luther believed the only true sacraments were those instituted by Christ in the Scriptures and accompanied by a physical sign. By this Reformed definition, Luther accepted only baptism and the Lord's Supper as valid sacraments. Pope Leo X excommunicated Luther from the Roman Catholic Church in January 1521.

But, not all Reformers agreed with all of Luther's ideas regarding the sacraments. In Zurich, Switzerland, the parish priest turned Protestant pastor, Ulrich Zwingli (1484-1531), criticized Luther for not going far enough in separating the Reformed view of the sacraments from Catholic teaching. He parted with Luther on baptism, teaching it was a rite of inclusion in the covenant people of God but not regenerative. And some of Zwingli's followers disagreed with the idea of baptizing infants. Zwingli also disagreed with Luther regarding the Lord's Supper; he denied the real presence of Christ in the bread and wine and viewed it as just a commemorative meal.

The Protestant pastor of the church in Geneva, Switzerland, John Calvin (1509-1564), taught that the two sacraments of the church—baptism and the Lord's Supper—are "signs and seals" of God's grace. For Calvin, baptism does not automatically save a person, it is a sign that God has accepted them into the church. Calvin parted with both Luther and Zwingli over their views of the Lord's Supper. Calvin saw the Lord's Supper as much more than Zwingli's commemorative meal, but he didn't agree with Luther or the Catholic church regarding the real presence of Christ; he taught that in the Supper, Christ is really present, but His presence is spiritual not physical.[1]

---

1. For more details of this brief historical sketch of the development of sacramental theology see: McGrath, *Christian Theology*, 419-444; Olson, *The Mosaic of Christian Belief*, 2002, 299-303; Shelley, *Church History in Plain Language*, 237-255.

By the time the Puritan clergy and theologians—often referred to as "divines"—gathered in London at Westminster Abbey to write the Westminster Confession of Faith in 1643, the reformation started by Martin Luther was more than one hundred years old. The Westminster divines had a wealth of Reformed theological scholarship to draw upon when formulating their Confession, including previous statements of faith, sermons, and the writings of many Reformed theologians, and their definition of a sacrament follows Calvin closely: "Sacraments are holy signs and seals of the covenant of grace . . . instituted by God along with that covenant to represent Christ and His benefits"[2] Following that definition, Reformed theologians recognize only baptism and the Lord's Supper as sacraments, they are both accompanied by a physical sign, they represent the covenant of grace, and they were clearly instituted by God in Christ.

In a covenant between God and humans, God establishes promises, commands, and penalties. In the first covenant God made with humans—the covenant of works—God commanded Adam and his wife to be fruitful and fill the earth, to subdue and rule over the rest of creation as stewards, and to observe a holy day of rest each week.[3] He also commanded Adam not to eat from the tree of the knowledge of good and evil. The penalty for breaking the covenant was death.[4]

The Bible tells us Adam, as the covenant head representing all of mankind, disobeyed God by eating fruit from the forbidden tree. Because Adam was unable to perfectly obey God, death entered the world. But Adam's fall did not disrupt God's eternal plan. God established a second covenant—the covenant of grace. The covenant of grace is God's promise of eternal life for those who have faith in the life, death, and resurrection of Jesus Christ;[5] their faith makes them right with God. It is a covenant of "grace" because what is promised—eternal life—is free and unmerited, even the faith that makes one right with God is a gift from God.[6] The sacraments, then, are physical signs that represent to our senses the death and resurrection of Jesus Christ, the washing away of sin, and rebirth into a new person who is right with God and promised eternal life in the covenant of grace.

2. WCF 27.1.
3. Genesis 1-2.
4. Genesis 2:17.
5. John 3:16; Romans 10:9.
6. Ephesians 2:8.

Part III: Sacraments

There is a close relationship between the physical sign of a sacrament and what the sign represents, but in Reformed theology the relationship is spiritual, not literal. The water of baptism does not literally wash sin off, and the bread and wine of the Lord's Supper are not literally the body and blood of Christ. Baptism allows us to visualize the spiritual cleansing that comes through faith in Christ. The bread and wine of the Lord's Supper help us to visualize and remember the broken body and the poured-out blood required of Christ for our salvation.

Reformed theologians also speak of sacraments as "seals," by which they mean a visible authentication. Like a seal on a government document confirming authenticity, sacraments are visible stamps of authenticity; they are reminders that God's promises are true and sure promises.

The sacraments are also ways that God establishes a visible distinction between the church and the world. In baptism, God marks a person as a member of His covenant family—the visible church—separate and distinct from the world. Likewise, the table of the Lord's Supper is a family table. It's where the covenant family of God comes to be in communion with Christ and with each other. Those who partake of the Supper are united to Christ by faith, and to each other as the body of Christ. The sacraments, then, make the church different from the world. They are a physical, lived-out way for the church to affirm God's promise. "They will be his people, and God himself will be with them and be their God."[7]

And, the sacraments are visible ways to show a commitment to the service of God in Christ. Like the Roman soldier's *sacramentum*, baptism and the Lord's Supper are ways for members of the church to pledge an oath of loyalty to Christ.

In the Reformed understanding, the sacraments do not have any inherent power; they do not save a person; salvation is by faith alone. And, simply saying the words of institution and applying water, or breaking bread and drinking wine, does not make the promises of baptism or the Lord's Supper take effect. But, the sacraments are important means of grace; when we participate in them God makes us more aware of His blessings and favor and that deepens our faith and increases our faithfulness as followers of Christ. The power and effectiveness of the sacraments comes from the work of the Holy Spirit through the Word of God instituting them to worthy receivers. A worthy receiver of the sacraments is not a person who has earned the right to receive a sacrament, it is a person who has the proper spirit of

---

7. Rev. 21:3.

faith, reverence, and repentance. When the Holy Spirit opens a person's heart to receive God's gift of saving faith, they trust in Christ and the Spirit comes to dwell within them, they are adopted into the family of God, and they are made worthy to receive the sacraments.

So, the efficacy of the sacraments does not depend on the people who receive them, or the people who administer them; it depends on the triune God; the Father gives authority to his Son, the Son institutes the sacraments, and the Holy Spirit applies them. The Holy Spirit applies the effect of the sacraments by working together with the Word of God to enable the believer to respond to the grace of the sacraments: "... you were washed, you were sanctified, you were justified in the name of the Lord Jesus Christ and by the Spirit of our God."[8] Therefore, the Reformers believed the sacraments must never be separated from the preaching of the Word, and only an ordained minister of the Word may properly administer the sacraments.

The two sacraments recognized in Reformed theology are the ones foreshadowed in the Old Testament rituals of circumcision and Passover. Christ, and His work of salvation, was hidden in the bread and wine of the Passover meal which was a sign of the shedding of blood for the forgiveness of sins, and it was replaced by the Lord's Supper in the New Testament. Similarly, circumcision, which in the Old Testament was a sign of entry into the covenant family of God and reception of the covenantal promises, was replaced by baptism in the New Testament. The Old Testament rituals and the New Testament sacraments are not identical, but their meanings are essentially the same.

Baptism

It is amazing to me that so much discord can result from a command so plain and simple as the command that Jesus gave to his disciples. "All authority in heaven and on earth has been given to me. Therefore, go and make disciples of all nations, baptizing them in the name of the Father and of the Son and of the Holy Spirit."[9] It seems straightforward, but for centuries Christians have disagreed about several issues related to baptism.

There are disagreements about who is to be baptized, when they are to be baptized, and how they are to be baptized. I don't have to look any further than my own family to see the range of baptismal interpretations

---

8. 1 Cor. 6:11.
9. Matt. 28:18-19.

that exist within Christianity. I was an infant baptized by pouring water on my head. My wife was an adult who was baptized by being fully immersed in a tub of water. My children were in elementary school when our pastor baptized them by sprinkling water on their heads. Which of these is the baptism that Jesus envisioned? Did he want us to baptize infants, children, adults, or all the above? Should a person be dunked, sprinkled, have water poured on them, or does it matter? If I was baptized as a baby, is it okay for me to be baptized again so that I can fully experience and remember it? What about people who are not baptized, is their salvation in question? The questions seem endless but, thankfully, there is one thing about baptism that all Christians agree on; it really is a sacrament!

In the Reformed tradition, baptism easily meets the requirements of a sacrament. Jesus Christ clearly institutes it at the end of Matthew's Gospel. It has a physical sign: water, which is related to the spiritual washing it signifies. It represents Christ and His benefits, including renewal or rebirth by the Holy Spirit, and cleansing from, or remission of sins. "He saved us through the washing of rebirth and renewal by the Holy Spirit."[10] It works as a seal authenticating the promises of the covenant of grace. And, it marks one as a member of the visible church, set apart from the world.

The physical sign of baptism is water which signifies the promises of the covenant of grace. Several times in the Bible we see God using water to separate His chosen covenant people from those who were opposed to Him and His people. The waters of the flood separated Noah and his family from an unbelieving world. The waters of the Red Sea separated Moses and the Israelites from Egyptians. With the water of baptism God marks His church as distinct from the world. The baptismal water is also a sign of ceremonial washing pointing to the covenant promise to wash away sin by the blood of Christ, forgiveness, and rising out of the water to new life by being united to Christ in His death and resurrection.

Jesus instructs the church to baptize in the name of the Father, Son, and Holy Spirit,[11] because baptism is administered by the authority of God, not man. And, Jesus commands the church to continue baptizing new disciples up until "the very end of the age."[12] But each disciple is baptized only once, by a minister of the gospel, because to re-baptize is to call into question the integrity of God's promises made in the first baptism. In baptism, God

---

10. Titus 3:5.
11. Matt. 28:19.
12. Matt. 28:20.

promises the indwelling Holy Spirit, union with Christ, remission of sins, and eternal life; to be baptized a second time is to repudiate the validity of God's promises and to ask God to make them again.

The Bible is clear that adults should be baptized when they come to faith in Christ and commit to follow Him. In the Book of Acts, we read the story of Philip sharing the gospel with an Ethiopian man traveling on the road from Jerusalem to Gaza. When the man came to faith he "gave orders to stop the chariot. Then both Philip and the eunuch went down into the water and Philip baptized him."[13] The Bible, however, is not explicit about whether or not infants and children should be baptized. Credible cases are made on both sides of the debate, and that debate has become overheated at times.

On January 17, 1525, the city council of Zurich, Switzerland, siding with the Reformer Ulrich Zwingli's belief in infant baptism, issued a decree that all parents who had neglected to have their children baptized must do so within a week or be banished from the city. But a group of Christians led by Conrad Grebel and Felix Manz refused to comply, believing instead that a person should be baptized only when they are capable of making a personal profession of faith in Jesus Christ. This group, the first Anabaptists, meaning "rebaptizers," not only defied the city government by not baptizing their children, they rebaptized any adult believer who had received the sacrament as an infant. To quash their disobedience, the city council doubled down and, on March 7, 1526, they passed an edict declaring that anyone who was caught rebaptizing would be put to death by drowning. The use of water to punish the defiant rebaptizers could not have been a coincidence. On January 5, 1527, Felix Manz became the first Anabaptist martyr, drowned in the Limmat River. Tragically, thousands more Anabaptists would be put to death across Europe during the early years of the Reformation for their "heretical" views of baptism.[14] Today, the descendants of the original Anabaptists include the various Mennonites, and their belief in adult baptism has been widely accepted by other Christians.

In Reformed theology, the case for baptizing infants and children of believing adults is built on scriptural evidence and the principle that the sacraments are intimately connected to the covenant of grace. In some cases, the Bible specifically mentions the children of believers who are being baptized. For example, on the day of Pentecost nearly two thousand years

---

13. Acts 8:38.
14. Shelley, 250-251.

ago, the apostle Peter preached a rousing sermon to a crowd in Jerusalem after which a number of people who heard him came to faith and wanted to be counted as committed followers of Christ. So, Peter instructed them, and their children, to be baptized. "Repent and be baptized, every one of you, in the name of Jesus Christ for the forgiveness of your sins. And you will receive the gift of the Holy Spirit. The promise is for you and your children and for all who are far off—for all whom the Lord our God will call."[15]

In other cases, the Bible mentions entire households being baptized which, presumably, would include children. For example, the apostle Paul shared the gospel with a woman named Lydia from the city of Thyatira. When she came to faith "she and the members of her household were baptized."[16] Also, late one night, Paul shared the gospel with the man who was guarding him in jail. The jailer came to faith and "immediately he and all his household were baptized."[17]

In addition to Scripture suggesting that children were being baptized in the first century church, the apostle Paul teaches that a believing parent has a sanctifying effect on their spouse and children. "For the unbelieving husband has been sanctified through his wife, and the unbelieving wife has been sanctified through her believing husband. Otherwise your children would be unclean, but as it is, they are holy."[18] Children who are "holy" are children who have been set apart as members of the covenant community and, in Paul's day, all members of the covenant community would be given the covenant sign. Therefore, it is likely that just as the covenant sign of circumcision was given to children in the Old Testament, the covenant sign of baptism was given to children in the New Testament. Baptizing infants and children of believing adult members of the covenant family of God maintains a historical continuity between Old Testament circumcision and New Testament baptism.

Finally, in support of infant baptism, Reformed theology looks back across the history of the church and finds the vast majority of Christians have baptized the children of believers. Records of infant baptism have been found going back to the middle of the second century. Some argue that infant baptism was the accepted norm across Christianity by the year 200 and, perhaps, that is why there is no history of controversy over it in

---

15. Acts 2:38-39.
16. Acts 16:15.
17. Acts 16:33.
18. 1 Cor. 7:14.

the ancient church. The assumption is that infant baptism was of apostolic origin and the silence on the issue in the New Testament speaks to its accepted practice.

Because baptism is a ceremonial, not actual washing, the amount of water used is not critical. A basis for full immersion, pouring, or sprinkling can be found in Scripture. Full immersion in water signifies burial with Christ and rising with Him to new life.[19] Pouring signifies the outpouring of the Holy Spirit.[20] The Reformed tradition favors sprinkling and its connection to the beautiful covenantal language in the Book of Ezekiel, "For I will take you out of the nations; I will gather you from all the countries and bring you back into your own land. I will sprinkle clean water on you, and you will be clean; I will cleanse you from all your impurities and from all your idols. I will give you a new heart and put a new spirit in you; I will remove from you your heart of stone and give you a heart of flesh. And I will put my Spirit in you and move you to follow my decrees and be careful to keep my laws"[21]

The Reformers did not view the sacraments, including baptism, as necessary for salvation because they insisted that we are made right with God through faith in Jesus Christ.[22] As far as we know, the criminal on the cross next to Jesus was saved without ever being baptized.[23] But the Reformed tradition does believe that baptism is essential for one's spiritual well-being. As a means of grace, baptism strengthens our faith in Christ and increases our assurance of God's love, whether we remember being baptized as an adult, or reflect back on the baptism we received as a child. Neglecting to be baptized when it is available is like saying "No thank you" to the grace God offers, and is living in disobedience to Jesus who commanded every new disciple to be baptized and instructed in the things He taught His disciples.

On the other hand, not every baptized person receives the covenantal promises and is saved. As was mentioned before, when God makes a covenant with humans He establishes promises and commandments, i.e., stipulations. The promises of the covenant of grace, signified by baptism, are based on the stipulation of faith—salvation is by faith alone. The church

19. Col. 2:12.
20. Titus 3:6.
21. Ezekiel 36:24-27.
22. Romans 3:22.
23. Luke 23:41-43.

baptizes to mark one as a person to whom the covenant promises and stipulations apply. The sign of entry into the covenant—the sacrament of baptism—is not a sign *of faith*, it is a sign of the *promises received by faith*. All of God's people should receive the sign and seal of His covenant promises, but the promises signified by baptism only become effective when, and if, a person believes and places their faith in Christ. Jesus spoke about some people who would profess belief and faith in Him and yet, to these same people, He would say, "I never knew you."[24] Some who are baptized based on a false profession of faith will never receive the promises of baptism.

Babies baptized before they believe are members of the visible church—the covenant people of God—and their baptism is a sign of God's covenant promises which remain for as many years as it may take for the child to grow up and come to faith; God cannot break a promise. When, and if, in God's perfect timing, the Spirit enables a baptized child to declare that Jesus is Lord, and they believe in their heart that God raised Him from the dead,[25] then God's promises: the remission of sin, rebirth, the indwelling of the Holy Spirit, and eternal life, signified by their baptism, take full effect.

Since the Scriptures are not explicit about infant versus adult baptism, perhaps the most important lesson we can glean from the Word of God on this topic is that we should not let this issue divide us as Christians.

The Lord's Supper

Hours before he was put to death Jesus shared a Passover meal with his disciples in a large upstairs guest room of a house in Jerusalem.[26] During the meal he thanked God for the bread, broke it, gave some of it to each of his disciples at the table, and made one of the most enigmatic statements anyone has ever made, "Take and eat; this is my body."[27] Then, later in the supper, he did it again. Taking a cup of wine, he said, "Drink from it, all of you. This is my blood of the covenant, which is poured out for many for the forgiveness of sins."[28] And with that, Jesus instituted the sacrament of the Lord's Supper, also called the Eucharist (Greek: *eucharistia*, meaning

---

24. Matt. 7:21-23.
25. Romans 10:9.
26. Luke 22:10-12.
27. Matt. 26:26.
28. Matt. 26:27-28.

"thanksgiving"), or communion (Latin: *communio*, meaning: "share in common"), one of the most controversial topics in the church.

Like baptism, the controversies surrounding this sacrament are not about whether it actually is a sacrament; from the earliest days of the church faithful followers of Christ gathered on the first day of the week to "break bread" together.[29] They were doing what Christ Himself had commanded: "do this in remembrance of me."[30] But how, exactly, were they doing it? Who was doing it? What was the meaning and purpose of what they were doing? These questions have not only created division between Protestants and Catholics; they have produced differing views of the Lord's Supper within the Reformed tradition as well. Luther, Calvin, and Zwingli each developed distinctive views of the Lord's Supper and followers of these men passed their views down through the centuries as is evident in the various beliefs of Protestant denominations today. The extent of the controversies and differences reflects the importance of the issue in the minds of Christians throughout the ages.

Chief among the differences is the debate over what Jesus meant when he said, "This is my body" in reference to the bread, and "This is my blood" in reference to the wine. Classical Reformed theology teaches that the words of Jesus were not to be taken literally; Jesus was using figurative language. This was a technique that Jesus had used before to reinforce His teaching. For example, He also said, "I am the light of the world,"[31] or "I am the gate,"[32] or "I am the true vine."[33] At the Last Supper, Jesus was saying, "I am this bread and this wine because this bread represents my body, and this wine represents my blood." Broken bread and poured-out wine were perfect signs of Jesus's broken body, and the blood He shed for the forgiveness of sins, both promised in the covenant of grace. In the mind of Calvin, and later the Westminster divines, the church erred when it tried to synthesize pagan philosophical ideas adopted from Aristotle, with Christian theology, in an attempt to explain what is simply figurative language. To the Reformers, the elaborate explanations were both unreasonable and unsupported by the Bible.

29. Acts 20:7.
30. Luke 22:19.
31. John 8:12.
32. John 10:9.
33. John 15:1.

Part III: Sacraments

At the Council of Chalcedon in 451 the Church's official definition of the incarnation of Christ was established: Jesus Christ is one person with two natures. The Council declared that Jesus is fully God and fully man, and the two natures are not mixed, confused, separated, or divided. Each of the two natures of Christ retains its own attributes. If our theology strays from this definition we are moving out of line with what has been established as orthodox Christianity, which is what Calvin argued both Luther and the Catholic church were doing.

From Calvin's perspective, the Catholic doctrine of transubstantiation, and the Lutheran doctrine of consubstantiation, both give a divine attribute to the human nature of Christ because they claim the body and blood of Christ are omnipresent. But, the Chalcedonian definition maintains that each nature retains its own attributes; the human nature does not become divine. The divine nature of Christ can be in heaven and, at the same time, always with us here on earth because the divine nature of Christ is omnipresent. But, the human nature of Christ is only in heaven, at the right hand of God the Father. If we hold on to the orthodox teaching of the two natures of Christ established at Chalcedon, the human nature of Christ cannot be in the Lord's Supper. The body and blood of Christ belong to His humanity, not to His deity, and His human nature is in heaven.

The classical Reformed view is that of Calvin, who argued there is a real presence of Christ in the Lord's Supper, but rejected the physical presence of Christ. In the Lord's Supper, Christ is really present, spiritually. And "spiritually" means much more than simply a feeling or thought; Christ is truly present in the Lord's Supper, in his divine nature. And so, in the Lord's Supper, we spiritually feed upon the risen Christ, just as the Israelites really, spiritually fed on Christ in the desert: "They all ate the same spiritual food and drank the same spiritual drink; for they drank from the spiritual rock that accompanied them, and that rock was Christ."[34]

Although the controversy over the real presence of Christ in the Lord's Supper has been divisive in church history, it seems we should be encouraged that there is agreement on the most important part of the debate: Reformed, Catholic, Lutheran, and Episcopalian theologians all believe that Christ really is present in the sacrament we call the Lord's Supper. The disagreements stem from "how" we understand that real presence. And because understanding how Christ is present leads us to the mystery of the incarnation and the dual nature of Christ—doctrines that are practically

---

34. 1 Cor. 10:3-4.

impossible for the human mind to fully comprehend—any discussion of this theological issue should probably begin with a healthy dose of awe, grace, and humility.

In the Reformed tradition the Lord's Supper has several purposes, one of which is to provide a powerful way for the church to remember Christ's death: "whenever you eat this bread and drink this cup, you proclaim the Lord's death until he comes."[35] In Jewish teaching, apostasy was closely related to forgetting. The people of Israel sinned against God when they forgot Him so, in order to always remember God and what He did for them, the Jewish calendar included several festivals and celebrations. Likewise, Christ gave His church a sacrament to be observed often and regularly, in order to remember that His body was broken, His blood was shed, He died to atone for our sins, He is with us always, and He has promised to come again.[36]

The sacrament is also a seal on our souls, a stamp of authenticity of the benefits of the cross of Christ. When we reflect on the sacrifice of Christ signified by the bread and wine we are reminded that by His wounds we are healed,[37] we have been redeemed from our enslavement to Satan, and we have been reconciled to God.

And because the Lord's Supper is a symbolic meal, it signifies spiritual nourishment. As bread and wine nourish the body, so the body and blood of Christ, spiritually consumed in the Supper, nourish the soul.

The sacrament is also a sign of commitment to Christ. In baptism we are marked as children of God, and in the Lord's Supper the covenant children of God commit to seek a deeper fellowship with Him. The more our mind reflects on the sacrament, the more our hearts are inflamed by Him, for Him.

In addition, the sacrament is a pledge of communion with Christ. Knowing that Christ is really—mystically and spiritually—present in the meal, we come to the Lord's table to be in communion with Him. And, the more we are in communion with Christ, the more the covenant of grace between God and us is strengthened: God promises to be our God, we promise to be His people.

Finally, the sacrament is a communion of the family. The kitchen or dinner table is where a family gathers for fellowship, and the table of the Lord's

---

35. 1 Cor. 11:26.
36. Matt. 24:44; 25:31.
37. 1 Peter 2:24.

Supper is where the covenant family of God comes together to share a meal, and to deepen their relationship with each other as the body of Christ.

As for who and how; Reformed theology views this sacrament as a ritual for believers who have been adopted into the covenant family of God. This requirement is not a way of establishing exclusivity, but it acknowledges that in the Supper we come into the real presence of Christ and so, we must be diligent to acknowledge the holiness of the ceremony. The apostle Paul warned against unbelievers participating in the Lord's Supper and against thoughtless believers who cavalierly participated in it. Paul says they not only negate the benefits of the sacrament, they could put themselves in real danger. "For those who eat and drink without discerning the body of Christ eat and drink judgment on themselves. That is why many among you are weak and sick, and a number of you have fallen asleep."[38]

Because the Bible refers to the Lord's Supper as a meal in which the covenant family joins in communion with each other and with Christ, "On the first day of the week we came together to break bread...,"[39] Reformed theologians believe it should not be administered privately. It should remain a very simple meal for the community, administered by a minister of the Word who uses the words of institution given by Christ to explain the meaning of the sacrament. Those receiving the sacrament receive both elements; a piece of bread and sample of wine (or non-alcoholic grape juice—fruit of the vine). In this simple ceremony the gospel is proclaimed, "God presented Christ as a sacrifice of atonement, through the shedding of his blood—fruit of the vine."[40]

Final Thoughts

To understand the divide between Reformed and Catholic theology with regard to the sacraments, we need to understand how the two traditions view the role of sacraments in our salvation. The Reformation was launched on the idea of *sola fide*: justification by faith alone, not justification by faith and sacraments. When the apostle John writes, "For God so loved the world that he gave his one and only Son, that whoever believes in him shall not perish but have eternal life,"[41] he did not say that whoever believes and

38. 1 Cor. 11:29-30.
39. Acts 20:7.
40. Romans 3:25.
41. John 3:16.

then is baptized, confirmed, confesses their sins to a priest, and receives communion, has eternal life. If being made right with God required participation in the sacraments we would be back to depending on a set of rules—the law—for our justification. But the apostle Paul said that is not the case: "So the law was our guardian until Christ came that we might be justified by faith."[42] As we discussed in Part Two, justification in Reformed theology happens the moment we come to faith. When we trust in Christ alone for the forgiveness of our sins, we can say with assurance that *we have been* saved. But at that very moment, a lifelong process of sanctification begins, so that we can also say, *we are being* saved. As a means of grace, the sacraments are not essential for our salvation, but they are very important in the ongoing process of our sanctification. As the Westminster Shorter Catechism puts it, the sacraments become effective means of salvation "by the blessing of Christ and the working of His Spirit in those who receive them by faith"[43]

---

42. Galatians 3:24.
43. WSC 91.

Part IV

Saints

*What Does Your Church Teach About
the Faithful Departed?*

Chapter 7

Sainthood

The Vocation of All Who Believe

Thomas M. Tasselmyer

The Reformed Protestant View

It was July 2, 1505, near the town of Stotternheim in central Germany, and 21-year-old Martin Luther was walking back to law school at the University in Erfurt after a visit home. As a thunderstorm moved in a bolt of lightning struck near Luther knocking him to the ground. Stunned and frightened, Luther blurted out a prayer, "Help me Saint Anne, I will become a monk!" This mostly likely was not Luther's first prayer to Saint Anne; his father was a successful businessman in the mining industry and therefore his family would have been very familiar with Saint Anne, the mother of Mary, and the patron saint of miners. And so, although it greatly disappointed his father who envisioned his son as a successful lawyer or judge, Luther interpreted his survival from the lightning bolt as a call from heaven leading him to the Augustinian monastery in Erfurt where he made the monastic vow that would change history.

Luther chose that particular monastery because its rule of religious life was known to be the most rigorous and therefore, Luther surmised, the most pleasing to God. In the monastery Luther worked as hard as humanly possible to find favor with God through prayer, fasting, daily confession, solitude, and vigils. He famously claimed that if ever a person could be made right with God and assure themselves a place in heaven through "monkery," he would have been the one to do it. But, his time in the monastery only convinced him of how he failed every day to keep the law of God perfectly; no one can live up to God's holy standards, no one can love God with all their heart, soul, mind, and strength, and love their neighbor as themselves. In the monastery Luther became fully aware that he could not reconcile his guilt with the holiness of God through human effort.

By divine providence, a lightning bolt and a prayer to a saint set in motion the monastic experience that would help Martin Luther formulate his understanding of salvation by faith alone upon which the Reformation was based. But, in the Reformed tradition that subsequently developed, the church does not canonize, venerate, or pray to saints. I believe a thoughtful and biblical basis for this approach to saints can be made, but at the same time I will admit that sometimes it seems like the Reformed tradition overreacts to anything dealing with saints. For example, most Reformed theologians will refer to "the apostle Paul" instead of "Saint Paul." That is quite interesting, when you think about it, since Paul almost certainly would have considered himself a "saint." It seems the fear of sounding too Catholic is the reason many Reformed theologians do not refer to the apostles and other biblical figures as saints. As a result, the Reformed tradition may be losing out on a rich tradition of the church.

I was reminded of this recently when listening to my daily prayer devotional while driving to work. I like to use an App on my phone called "Pray as You Go" which was designed by a group of British Jesuits based on the spirituality of Saint Ignatius of Loyola. Each day's devotional begins with the narrator marking the day, date, and current point on the church calendar. Last week, the narrator caught my attention when the prayer began with "Today is Thursday, the 21st of September, the Feast of Saint Matthew, in the 24th week of Ordinary Time." Our youngest son is named Matthew. To hear that day marked as a Feast Day for Saint Matthew, and to be reminded that the name Matthew means "Gift of God," inspired me to pray for our Matthew. I was reminded to pray that our Matthew would mature in his faith, and to be thankful to have him as a son; a real gift of God. And I was reminded that our Matthew is one of many Matthews who have believed in Christ and joined a great communion of saints. A prayer App designed by Reformed theologians might have missed that, even though the Reformed tradition does acknowledge the existence of saints. The Reformation principle of *Sola Scriptura* demands that we look to the

Bible when developing our theology, and the Bible, after all, does speak of saints and even teaches us to look to them for inspiration.

Definition of a Saint

One of the apostle Paul's favorite names for the people he was writing to in the churches at Rome, Corinth, Ephesus, Philippi, Colossae, or Thessalonica, comes from the Greek word *hagios* which, in most English Bibles, is translated "saints." For example, his letter to the Ephesians begins, ". . . to the saints who are in Ephesus, and are faithful in Christ Jesus . . ."[1] Paul considered all believers who professed a faith in Christ to be saints. In fact, according to Paul, God has called every Christian to be a saint. He begins his letter to the church in Rome with, "To all those in Rome who are loved by God and *called to be saints* . . ."[2] So, if Paul were preaching at my church this Sunday he might greet the congregation with, "Good morning, saints of Hunt Valley Church!" However, he probably would not greet any of us individually at Hunt Valley Church as "Saint Tom," or "Saint Laurie," etc., because that would require knowledge of what is in our hearts.

There could be, and in fact we hope there are, people in our churches who are seeking Christ but who have not yet placed their faith in Him. We view our mission at Hunt Valley Church as one that reaches all people with the gospel, so we hope there are guests and visitors who are not yet "saints," by Paul's definition, joining us each Sunday. Additionally, we cannot presume that even those who worship with us regularly are saints. Jesus described the people who populate the kingdom of God as a mixture of "wheat and weeds,"[3] that is, a mixture of true believers and others who are not believers. And He said some in the church will do very saintly things in His name: prophesy, drive out demons, perform miracles; but not even all of them will be saints. To some of them He will say, "I never knew you. Away from me, you evildoers!"[4]

---

1. Ephesians 1:1. I am using the English Standard Version (ESV) translation because the updated, 2011 New International Version (NIV), which I reference throughout most of this book, decided to change their translation of *hagios* from "saints" to "God's holy people." Very disappointing to me!
2. Romans 1:7, ESV, emphasis added.
3. Matt. 13:24-30.
4. Matt. 7:23.

Part IV: Saints

Our assurance comes from knowing what is in our own heart, but we cannot make that judgment about others. We may observe others professing their faith in Christ and living in accordance with that profession, they may even do genuinely good, if not miraculous deeds, but only God knows who He has called to be a saint. That may be why, in the New Testament, the Greek word *hagios* is used to refer to saints (plural), not any individual saint. The church is comprised of many saints, but their outward actions are not what merit sainthood; it is a matter of the heart.

Thankfully, the Bible does reveal to us saints—people with a heart of true faith—on whose shoulders the church stands. Inspired by the Holy Spirit, the apostle Paul writes, "I am the very least of all the saints."[5] Jesus prays to his Father in heaven and indicates that only one of His disciples was "lost."[6] Therefore, we may conclude that, except for Judas who betrayed Jesus, the other eleven disciples kept the faith and are truly saints. Jesus also said, "Greater love has no one than this: to lay down one's life for one's friends. You are my friends if you do what I command."[7] The martyrs of the church who have laid down their lives out of love for Jesus are surely saints. The Virgin Mary is clearly a saint, having found favor with God.[8] And, the great hall of fame of faith found in chapter eleven of the Book of Hebrews lists numerous people we can be sure are saints, including Abel who was "commended as righteous,"[9] Enoch who did not die but was taken away because he "pleased God,"[10] and Noah who "became heir of the righteousness that is in keeping with faith."[11] But, other than the apostles, martyrs, and those the Bible identifies as saints, we are only conjecturing when we attempt to canonize people and set them apart because, no matter how saintly they appear to be, we cannot know a person's heart and whether they are a person of true saving faith. Therefore, let's gather together as a community of Christ followers to worship, pray, learn, and enjoy fellowship with one another assuming we are all saints—our professions of faith

---

5. Ephesians 3:8, ESV.
6. John 17:12.
7. John 15:13-14.
8. Luke 1:28ff.
9. Hebrews 11:4.
10. Hebrews 11:5.
11. Hebrews 11:7.

are genuine—and let God sort out what recognition and rewards we will receive when Christ returns.[12]

Veneration and Prayer

In the Reformed tradition veneration of the saints is not practiced. From a purely logical standpoint, as stated above, outside of the biblical witness we cannot truly know who the individual saints are. But even when it comes to the saints made known to us in the Bible, e.g. Matthew, Mark, John, Peter, Mary, etc., there are theological reasons for not venerating them as well.

In the Bible, God frequently tells us that He is a jealous God. Nothing is more perfect in love, wisdom, power, holiness, justice, goodness, and truth than God. Therefore, it is not only right, but also good that God commands all honor and worship is to be to Him alone.[13] God's jealous nature means that He is zealous for His people. There is a bond between God and His people as exclusive as a marriage bond. As a husband should be zealous for his wife, so God is zealous for His people. When we venerate a creature, we give it what only God deserves, and we move dangerously close to idolatry which is tantamount to spiritual adultery. Reformed theology steers clear of venerating creatures because it can break the bond between God and His people.

Jesus set the standard when He was tempted in the desert. Satan offered Jesus "the kingdoms of the world" if He would simply worship him, but Jesus refused. "Away from me, Satan! For it is written: 'Worship the Lord your God, and serve him only.'"[14] Jesus is clear that we must avoid literally, or even figuratively, putting ourselves in a position of paying religious homage, reverence, or adoration to anyone other than God.

It can be very hard to discern the difference between the kind of worship that Jesus spoke against and the veneration of saints. We are walking a razor thin line between what is acceptable to God and what is idolatry when we try to make a distinction between venerating and worshiping something other than God. Even the apostle John (a saint himself!), was rebuked for crossing that line when he desired to worship a creature, "I fell down to worship at the feet of the angel . . . But he said to me, 'Don't do that!

---

12. Rev. 22:12.
13. Exodus 20:5.
14. Matt. 4:8, 10.

Part IV: Saints

I am a fellow servant with you and with your fellow prophets and with all who keep the words of this scroll. Worship God!'"[15]

The story of Peter and Cornelius in chapter ten of the Book of Acts, however, is most instructive for me. We know the apostle Peter is a saint. His faith was tested at times, such as when he tried to walk on water with Jesus,[16] or when a servant girl in the courtyard of Caiaphas the high priest identified him as a follower of Jesus and he denied even knowing Jesus.[17] But through it all, Peter remained one of the eleven disciples that Jesus himself said was not lost; he was a man of true saving faith and therefore a true saint. Cornelius was a God-fearing Gentile—he worshiped the one true God with the Jews—and he was a well-respected man of prayer. Following the directions given to him by an angel of God, Cornelius sent for Peter, and when he arrived, "Cornelius met him and fell at his feet in reverence. But Peter made him get up; "'Stand up,' he said, 'I am only a man myself.'"[18] Think about that scene. Cornelius was admonished to not show reverence to a true, living saint standing right in front of him. It seems to me there is no practical difference between the reverence Cornelius wanted to show Peter, and veneration of Peter, or any other saint. The real lesson here, from Saint Peter himself, is that we are not to venerate anything or anyone other than God, not even the most impressive saints. As John Calvin put it, "Let it suffice to remember, that whatever offices of piety are bestowed anywhere else than on God alone, are of the nature of sacrilege."[19]

Likewise, in the Reformed tradition there are theological reasons for not praying to, or through saints.[20] The Bible is clear about who it is that brings our prayers to our Father in heaven. "For there is one God and one mediator between God and mankind, the man Christ Jesus."[21] And, as our eternal High Priest, Jesus is continually making intercession for us.[22] Therefore, you cannot be more confident that your prayers will be heard and, yes,

---

15. Rev. 22:8-9.
16. Matt. 14:28-30.
17. Matt. 26:69-75.
18. Acts 10:25-26.
19. Calvin, *Institutes of the Christian Religion* 1.12.3, trans. Henry Beveridge, 63.
20. I appreciate Lyle's portion of this section clarifying the difference between praying "to" and praying "with" saints.
21. 1 Tim. 2:5.
22. Hebrews 7:25.

answered, than when you pray in the name of Jesus. "You may ask me for anything in my name, and I will do it."[23]

Of course, this isn't magic. Prayers lifted to God through the intercession of Jesus are always heard and answered, but we must realize that sometimes the answer will be "no," or "not yet." Other times, however, when we pray in His name—in accordance with His perfectly holy will—the answer is "yes."

But no matter the answer, it doesn't seem wise to petition a saint when Jesus is ready, willing, and telling us to come to Him with our prayers. I imagine not going directly to Jesus with our prayers might even be disappointing to Him.

Furthermore, Jesus referred to Himself as the bridegroom and the church as His bride. That means our relationship with Jesus should be as close and intimate as a marriage relationship. In a marriage we don't ask a third party to communicate our deepest longings, fears, concerns, or needs to our spouse for us. If we love and trust our spouse, we want to personally communicate our thoughts and feelings to them. In fact, it is not hard to imagine how we might inflame the righteous jealousy of God when we do not come to Him through Christ alone with our prayers.

Life After Death

Part of grappling with the concept of praying for the faithfully departed saints involves understanding our theology of death. Do the saints who have died need our prayers? Based on what Scripture seems to say, and not say, the Reformed tradition answers, "No."

It is a real shame that no one in the first century church interviewed Jesus's good friend, Lazarus, and recorded for posterity what he had to say about the "first" time he died. What a missed opportunity! Here was a man who was in the grave longer than Jesus. The apostle John tells us Lazarus had been dead for four days before Jesus arrived and brought him back to life![24] John includes the story in his Gospel (maybe he did interview Lazarus?), but it would have been nice to hear from Lazarus himself. Surely, he could have provided us with some insights and practical tips for facing what the apostle Paul calls "the last enemy," i.e., death.[25]

---

23. John 14:14.
24. John 11:39.
25. 1 Cor. 15:26.

Part IV: Saints

Although we don't have the eyewitness testimony of Lazarus, the Bible is not silent about death and what happens after we die. Under the inspiration of the Holy Spirit, New Testament writers gave us an account of the death and resurrection of Jesus, which is actually a better example of what each of us will experience than whatever Lazarus experienced. After all, poor Lazarus was dead, then was raised to life, and then had to continue aging and eventually die a second time. We, on the other hand, will only die once and then, like Jesus, we will receive a resurrection body that doesn't age. "For if we have been united with him in a death like his, we will certainly also be united with him in a resurrection like his."[26]

In addition to the example of Jesus's death and resurrection, the apostles passed on to us what Jesus had taught them about dying and the life to come. Therefore, Paul says the church doesn't have to be like the rest of the world, uninformed and without hope when contemplating death.[27] Paul passes along to us what he learned "according to the Lord's word . . . ,"[28] and what the Lord taught is good news indeed, that ". . . Jesus died and rose again, and so we believe that God will bring with Jesus those who have fallen asleep in him."[29] So, while the Reformers couldn't address all the questions we might have, they were able to tap into the Scriptures and construct a fairly robust understanding of what happens when our life on earth has ended.

Death was not originally a part of God's creation. But, God did warn Adam about the possibility of death. He told Adam not to eat from one particular tree in the garden: ". . . you must not eat from the tree of the knowledge of good and evil, for when you eat from it you will certainly die."[30] When Adam disobeyed God, death entered the world and the fate of our bodies was set. "By the sweat of your brow you will eat your food until you return to the ground, since from it you were taken; for dust you are and to dust you will return."[31] Ever since Adam fell into sin, when a person dies their body decomposes and returns to dust, just as God established.

While our bodies return to dust, our souls return to God: ". . . the dust returns to the ground it came from, and the spirit returns to God who gave

26. Romans 6:5.
27. 1 Thess. 4:13.
28. 1 Thess. 4:15.
29. 1 Thess. 4:14.
30. Genesis 2:17.
31. Genesis 3:19.

it."[32] Reformed theology rejects the teaching of the Greek philosophers who believed human souls are inherently immortal. Instead, they understood the Scriptures to say human souls are created, not eternal. Our created souls depend on our Creator to exist. God preserves our souls and the life of our souls depends on His power: "... in him all things were created ... and in him all things hold together."[33] When we die, our souls do not die, nor do they sleep; our personal life goes on in what Reformed theology calls the intermediate state. In the intermediate state our souls exist without a physical body.

The apostle Paul spoke of the intermediate state as far better than what we experience now. In his letter to the Christians in Philippi he said, "I am torn between the two: I desire to depart and be with Christ, which is better by far; but it is more necessary for you that I remain in the body."[34] How is the intermediate state "better by far"? The souls of believers in the intermediate state are perfected in holiness, that is, they are glorified and made unable to sin. They are received into heaven and behold the face of God: the beatific vision. They experience the ultimate joy and delight that all Christians are promised, "Blessed are the pure in heart, for they will see God."[35] The intermediate state, however, is just that: intermediate, not the end, and not the best. The best comes with the final resurrection when the souls of believers who have died are reunited with their glorified bodies.

For the souls of unbelievers, however, a different fate awaits. The intermediate state for them is not better by far. For them, the intermediate state is hell—a tormenting darkness where the Light of the world, Christ, is not seen. Unbelievers and fallen angels will not see the Light, the face of God in Christ. "And the angels who did not keep their positions of authority but abandoned their proper dwelling—these he has kept in darkness, bound with everlasting chains for judgment on the great Day."[36]

In Reformed theology, heaven and hell are the only two places for souls after death. The Reformers, unable to find a source for it in Scripture, did not accept the idea of purgatory. They also did not ascribe to the belief that further purging is necessary after death. For them, Christ's atonement

32. Ecclesiastes 12:7.
33. Col. 1:16-17.
34. Philippians 1:23-24.
35. Matt. 5:8.
36. Jude 6.

on the cross was itself the perfect purging. "For by one sacrifice he has made perfect forever those who are being made holy."[37]

Through faith in Christ our sins are forgiven, the penalty for those sins is paid in full, a life of becoming Christ-like by the power of the Holy Spirit dwelling in us begins, and our glorification when we die is assured. Glorified, beholding the face of God, and in paradise, saints experience eternity on God's time, "With the Lord a day is like a thousand years, and a thousand years are like a day."[38] The Bible doesn't give us all the answers to all the questions inquiring minds conjure up, only what God has determined we should know. "The secret things belong to the Lord our God, but the things that are revealed belong to us and to our children forever . . . ,"[39] but I think it's fair to presume that what we call "time" does not exist in heaven. And so, it may be that the saints who have gone before us will literally have no time to pray for us because time does not exist for them. I cannot prove it, but I suspect our loved ones, and all the saints who went home to God before us, will greet us in paradise after our death as if no time at all had separated us.

Final Thoughts

The divide between Reformed and Catholic theology with respect to saints seems to stem largely from the way the two traditions define a saint. In Reformed theology a saint is anyone who has received God's gift of saving faith. Therefore, sainthood is not merited, it is given; saints are not canonized, they are recognized; and saints are not venerated or prayed to, they are celebrated because they inspire the church and bring glory to God. The great cloud of witnesses that the writer of the Book of Hebrews refers to are the saints that went before us and still surround us in the unseen world. They are the saints who now motivate us to "throw off everything that hinders and the sin that so easily entangles," who push us on to "run with perseverance the race marked out for us," not so that they will be glorified as super-Christians, but so that we will always be "fixing our eyes on Jesus" and He will be glorified.[40]

Seen this way, I believe the Reformed tradition could, and should embrace a more robust theology of saints, one that brings depth to what we say

37. Hebrews 10:14.
38. 2 Peter 3:8.
39. Deuteronomy 29:29.
40. Hebrews 12:1-2.

when reciting the Apostles' Creed: "I believe in the communion of saints." We should not be timid about remembering, honoring, and being inspired by the saints who have gone before us. And we should always remember that the church consists of a communion of believers—saints—with each saint united to Jesus Christ and therefore to each other. In the church, the saints commune in worship, the sacraments, the Word, and prayers. When the saints gather for worship they glorify God and comfort each other. The saints also build each other up in bible studies, prayer, small groups, and mentoring. And, each saint brings individual gifts and graces for the mutual good of the church. Together the saints form the body of Christ on earth and no part of the body—no saint—is more important than another. In fact, "God has put the body together, giving greater honor to the parts that lacked it, so that there should be no division in the body, but that its parts should have equal concern for each other. If one part suffers, every part suffers with it; if one part is honored, every part rejoices with it."[41]

---

41. 1 Cor. 12:24-26.

Chapter 8

Saints

Models of Discipleship

Lyle K. Weiss

The Saints Were and Are Human Beings

During a trip to Cleveland with friends several years ago, we paid a visit to the Rock and Roll Hall of Fame. Though somewhat disappointed by the presence of groups who do not represent the rock 'n' roll genre of music, it was nevertheless an enjoyable and informative visit. Most memorable for me personally was the viewing of a video presentation concerning drugs, alcohol, and the rock 'n' roll lifestyle. During the video, Pete Townshend, legendary guitarist for the rock group The Who, spoke of the price paid for the seeming omnipresence of drugs in the world of rock music. In language significantly saltier than would be appropriate for this volume, Townshend lamented the loss of many friends and colleagues over the years to drugs. "They may be your . . . icons and heroes but they were my friends and now they're dead. They were people I loved and enjoyed playing with and now they're dead." We can look back on the legends of rock through misty eyes envisioning the glories of a life in rock and roll, all the while forgetting these men and women were living, breathing human beings with parents, siblings, spouses, children, and friends who loved them deeply and missed them just as deeply and enduringly once they were gone.

I am often reminded of the danger of forgetting the humanity of the heroes who have gone before us. My son and I enjoy visiting the Gettysburg Battlefield a couple of times a year. Usually on a Saturday morning, we set out early for the hour-long drive to Pennsylvania resulting in the opportunity to spend the day among the statues, monuments, and memorials as we walk the ground hallowed by the deeds of those who fought there and the immortal words of a president who powerfully reminded us why the war was being fought. As is so often the case when one explores significant events in history generally and, for my son and I, the American Civil War, it is easy to forget that for the men who battled on those fields the outcome of the war and the direction of the nation was still very much in doubt. My son and I walk the ground knowing that the Union won the battle and the war, forever cementing in the American identity the two goals attained by the conflict. First, the war affirmed Jefferson's timeless words in the Declaration of Independence that all people are created equal and second, it confirmed the indivisible bond that unites us as a nation and as a people. But, those men represented by the statues that dot the field did not know any of that. We may have turned them into marble objects of reverence but it is vital that we recall they were all too human, ordinary people who were able to rely on their strengths and minimize their weaknesses as they struggled to defend the nation against those who would have sundered it in two.

The willingness to remember the humanity of those who have gone before us is vital not only for appreciating the contributions and losses of those in the world of rock and roll or the American Civil War. It is essential if we are to develop and maintain our appreciation for the saints in the Roman Catholic tradition. Too often, like Civil war heroes or rock and roll icons, we have relegated the saints to the world of marble, forgetting their humanity and limiting their power to move and inspire us by removing them from the challenges and struggles, joys and thrills of human existence. Often forgotten in their marble life is the fundamental fact that they were, like us, ordinary human beings striving to live the gospel in the complicated time and place in which they lived. We can look back in hindsight on the American Civil War and see how everything worked together to achieve the right outcome. It looks so simple and clear. So, too, with the saints we can look at their lives and see how clear God's call was and how following the path they chose was so obvious. And yet, God's call was no clearer to them than it is to us. The path to follow was no more obvious to them than ours is to us. Our easy willingness to make of them marble men and women too often results in a diminishment of our appreciation of their humanity. And through the diminishment of their humanity, we limit their power to move and inspire us today.

Despite this tendency through the years to gloss over the humanity of the saints by an unnecessary and oftentimes unhealthy focus on the mystical and supernatural, the saints continue to exert their greatest influence on the believing community precisely through their humanity. The stories we sometimes tell of them, in an effort to emphasize their closeness with God, often have the unintended consequence of distancing them from the rest of humanity, from the rest of us. If one of the main gifts the saints provide the church is their function as role models, that very gift is undercut by the chasm created by an unwitting focus on their superhuman or otherworldly qualities. Who would believe they could walk in the footsteps of believers whose faith and holiness is so far beyond that of ordinary women and men? What makes them worthy of our veneration and attention is their willingness, despite the uncertainties, struggles, and ambiguities of life, to give themselves to God, heeding the Lord's call to follow him.

But, despite periodic efforts to dismiss the significance of the saints in Catholic thought and life, it remains true that the saints continue to be valuable members of the believing community. To understand the place of the saints in Catholic thought and life requires an understanding of certain elements of Catholic ecclesiology, the theological study of the church. What this chapter will offer is a view of the church which holds that saints continue to be members, will make distinctions between canonized and non-canonized saints, affirm the role of saints as intercessors, and articulate the enduring power of the saints to serve the community in every age as role models, supporting believers in their efforts to live the gospel life. In this role, the church has always afforded Mary the Mother of God a unique place of honor among the saints. Mary's place in the church has long been a source of confusion and disagreement so we shall endeavor to sort out the issues and offer some reflections on Mary's importance in the life of the church.

Who Are the Saints

Before we discuss the role of the saints in the life of the church, we should first say a word about who we mean when we use the word saints. In the same vein as Tradition and tradition, Scripture and scripture, Sacraments and sacraments, the church affirms the existence of Saints and saints. The term saint acts at three distinct levels. First, the church is the assembly of all the saints, living and dead, who form the one body of Christ. Formed, governed, and guided by the Holy Spirit, a basic definition of the church is the communion of saints. Second, the term saint can refer to those believers whose lives have been a clear expression of the love of God but have not received official sanction from the church's governing bodies. Throughout our lives, we may cross paths with holy men and women who are never officially declared saints by the church but whose lives are nevertheless a powerful witness to gospel fidelity and divine love. It may be a member of our very own family, a next-door neighbor, a public figure, a beloved teacher, or the person sitting to our right or left at Sunday mass or in the movie theater. Regardless of their link to us, they are nevertheless a stunning example of a life well-lived, of a life lived in fidelity to the gospel by someone who was willing to do God's will in God's way. Whether they are ever recognized as such by the church, they remain saints to those who knew them.

The third level of the term saint refers to those women and men who, throughout the history of the church, have been recognized by the official decree of the believing community to be saints. Their lives were such a transparent embodiment of the love of Christ that the church professes in faith that upon their deaths they entered directly into the eternal presence and love of God. Prior to the year 1234, the church did not have a formal process for the identification of saints. But, as is often the case, misuse and abuse created the need to develop a more formal process. For example, a monk in Sweden was named a saint after he was killed in a drunken brawl. Such behavior hardly identified the monk as a martyr but he was named a saint nevertheless. In the year 1234 Pope Gregory IX established formal procedures for the determination of official sainthood. Though the process has changed over the centuries and the name of the office that handles applications has changed, given the importance of saints in the life of the church, the church deems it necessary for the community to examine the lives of those being put forward for sainthood.

As it proceeds today, the process begins when a person dies who has what is called either 'fame of sanctity' or 'fame of martyrdom.' Fame of sanctity means the reputation for having lived an exemplary life of faith and fame of martyrdom refers to the person dying for the sake of Christ and his gospel. The bishop of the local diocese or archdiocese initiates the investigation, primarily examining two facets of the person's life. First, has any special favor or miracle been granted through the person's intercession?

Second, are their writings pure, true to the church's proclamation of the gospel and devoid of anything heretical? If both of these are found to be true, then the information is submitted to the Vatican's Congregation for the Causes of the Saints. If the person's cause is accepted, the Congregation investigates the person further. While this investigation proceeds, a devil's advocate is appointed for the purpose of raising objections and doubts. These objections and doubts must be resolved. If this investigation determines that the person died for the faith or lived a life of exemplary virtue, the person can be declared 'Venerable.'

Having been named 'Venerable,' the next phase of the process involves Beatification. A person may be declared beatified on the basis of martyrdom alone. If not, the person must be credited with a miracle. It must be determined by the church that the miracle was performed in response to the intercession of the person. If a person is beatified, they may be venerated but the veneration must be limited, perhaps to a particular region or to a particular religious order. After beatification comes canonization. In order for the person to be canonized, another miracle must be confirmed. Once confirmed, the person may be named a saint. Though the church maintains its standards given the fact that the saints remain powerful examples for the faithful in every age, some critics suggest too much weight is placed upon miracles in the process. In response, the church would suggest the miracles affirm the presence of the person with God and therefore affirm the goodness of their lives and the faithfulness of their discipleship. Critics of the process often suggest far too many believers who led lives of heroic fidelity are not considered because of the absence of miracles. Further, they would point out far too many saints are clergy and religious, failing to rightfully acknowledge the exemplary faith of the laity in every age. Pope John Paul II certainly began an effort to right this imbalance but much remains to be done.

These are the three ways in which the term saint can often be used in the church. For the purposes of this chapter, we will be focusing upon the second and third meanings of the term and title.

The Church

In the Roman Catholic vision of the church, the community of faith is not bound by time or place. It does not matter if you live down under in Australia, in sub-Saharan Africa, or if you are an inhabitant of a red or blue state in the United States. There are no boundaries limiting inclusion in the believing community. As St. Paul affirmed in his Letter to the Galatians, "As many of you as were baptized into Christ have clothed yourselves with Christ. There is no longer Jew or Greek, there is no longer slave or free, there is no longer male and female; for all of you are one in Christ Jesus."[1] Time, place, ethnicity, gender, or status are no longer barriers to inclusion among the people of God. Even death is not a barrier to inclusion in the church. Whether you were a Punic laborer in the fourth century, a peasant in the 12th, an American president in the twentieth century, or a member of the original 12, each belonged, and belongs, to the same church. Death did not interrupt their membership or jettison them from the body of Christ. Rather, all believers, living and dead, belong to the church and nothing, not death nor life in Paul's memorable phrases, can separate us from Christ.[2] Through the celebration of the sacraments of initiation discussed in the previous chapter, the believer is incorporated into the life of Christ and into the life of the believing community, indelibly marked as belonging to Christ and his church forever.

To speak of the saints in the Roman Catholic tradition then is not to speak solely of the past, to envision the saints as former members of the community who can offer insight and wisdom to the current occupants of the church. That the saints are clearly women and men of their own time is a given. When Francis reflected upon and prayed for peace, he did so without knowledge of the threat of nuclear war or terrorism. Saints too often adopted the views of their society regarding women, slavery, authority, and status. Saints were not perfect people. Whatever faults and sins their cultures and societies embodied at the times they sometimes accepted and absorbed into their own identities. We cannot appreciate their greatness by hiding from the ugly truths visible in their complexity. But, far more than others, they remained faithful to the gospel and embodied courage in the face of the obstacles, dangers, and threats they encountered while striving to remain faithful amidst the vicissitudes of their own age.

But, even as they are truly people of their own times and places, people of a past age, they nevertheless remain people of the present moment as well. They will always be people of the present because death did not sunder their relationship with the church but offered them the opportunity to be continuously present to it in every succeeding generation. To speak of the saints for Roman Catholics is to appreciate the presence of these holy

1. Galatians 3:27-28.
2. Romans 8:31-39.

women and men still among us. Though for the moment their presence with us may be veiled, they are nevertheless present just as Christ is present though no longer in the human form he once occupied while living in ancient Israel proclaiming the reign of God. Accepting a broad definition of the church allows us to understand both the past and present forms of the saints and helps us appreciate their current role as both intercessors and as role models for the faithful.

Praying with the Saints

One of the great misunderstandings of the Roman Catholic tradition, particularly regarding saints, is the widespread belief that Catholics pray to saints. This belief is widespread due in large part to the actions and words of Roman Catholics themselves, who may or may not understand their own tradition on this issue or who may simply fail to appreciate the nuance of language. In the Catholic tradition, believers pray primarily to God the Father though it may also be directed to Jesus and the Holy Spirit. We most often address the Father in prayer but do so through Christ in the Spirit.[3] We do not pray to saints. Rather, we pray with saints. The easiest way to express our belief in the validity of praying with the saints is to cite a very common Christian experience. When either we or someone we know is going through a difficult time, we will often reach out to friends and family, to members of our faith community and ask that they pray for us or for our loved one. Though Christians of all stripes make this request quite often, and quite unthinkingly, some of those same Christians balk at the Catholic notion of praying with the saints. This is one practical application of the Catholic belief in the broadness of the church. The saints are no less a part of the believing community than the people sitting to our right and left at liturgy. We would, without any trepidation, ask that they pray for us, for our loved one, or for a particularly difficult situation in our life or in the life of the world. When Catholics pray with the saints, we engage in the same custom grounded in the belief in the power of prayer. We may ask the saints to intercede for us but, given their continuing inclusion in the church community, that is no different than requesting a fellow believer intercede for us to God. Their closeness to God provides us with confidence in the efficacy of our prayer to God.

---

3. Catechism of the Catholic Church, 2663-2672.

In Steven Spielberg's powerful film 'Munich,' an Israeli Mossad agent is speaking with his mother about the role he played in bringing the architects of the terrorist attack on Israeli athletes at the Olympic Games in Munich, Germany, to justice. His mother speaks with him about her past, about how most of her family were killed by the Nazis before and during the Second World War, about how she came to Israel alone, and how she prayed to have a son. In her recollection, she mentions her memory of climbing a hill overlooking Jerusalem to pray and recalls how she felt her deceased family members there, praying with her. The dead were with her as she prayed. The dead are still with us, albeit in a veiled way. They are companions of the living in our shared journey to the fulfillment of God's kingdom. Just as her ancestors were with her to pray for the blessings of a new life in Jerusalem, so too are the saints with us to pray for our needs and concerns, to share our joys and sorrows, and to intercede for us with God.

Patron Saints

Most Christians are familiar with the term patron, as in patron saint. A saint can be the patron of a church, a region, a nation, a trade, or any number of experiences and endeavors related to human existence. A patron is one who is considered a special intercessor with God. According to Merriam Webster, a patron refers to a person chosen, named, or honored as a special guardian, protector, or supporter, as in a patron of the arts. A patron often uses financial or other means to support and advocate for a cause, an organization, an institution, or an individual. A patron saint is a person chosen or elected to serve as an intercessor in support of a church, a diocese or archdiocese, a nation, a trade, or other human experience. For example, the patron saint of the United States is Mary, under the title of Immaculate Conception. Individual churches are named for the saints who offer special support for the community. St. Joseph, St. Michael, St. Louis, St. Francis, St. Catherine, and St. Teresa are just a few examples of the myriad possibilities. St. Albertus Magnus is the patron saint for natural scientists, St. Damian is the patron for doctors and surgeons, St. Patrick is the patron for engineers, and St. Sebastian is the patron for soldiers just to cite a few examples of patrons of particular professions. St. Crescentinus is the patron of those who suffer from headaches, St. Florian is invoked against fire, floods, and drowning, Macrina the Elder is the patron of those who suffer poverty, and Potomiana is the patron of those who have been raped. If there is a church, a region, a trade, or a human experience, a saint can be given the title of patron to serve as guardian, protector, or supporter of those living in that region, worshipping in that church, working in that field, or sharing in that human experience.

The concept of a patron is built upon the notion that the saints remain members of the living, breathing community of faith. The selection of the particular patron has depended on various elements. For instance, does the church, region, or nation have possession of the saint's body or some important relic of the saint; did the person announce the gospel to that particular area or nation; did the saint die in that region; did the founder of the church have a special devotion to the saint; does the saint embody a particular virtue or exhibit a specific charism that is needed for a particular community or industry? These and other elements are part of the decision to name a patron. The tradition of holy relics is of particular note since many may be familiar with the Catholic tradition of burying relics of the saints in the altars of churches. This tradition of burying relics, usually parts of the saint's body, has its origin in the earliest days of the Christian church when liturgies were celebrated on the tombs of the martyrs. The burial places of saints were considered sacred places where the community would gather for worship. As the church moved into more peaceful times, the custom of performing liturgies on the graves of the saints continued. Even to this day, altars in Catholic churches have buried within them relics of the saints as a reminder of our beginnings when we would pray on the entombed bodies of the saints. Though, as often happens, superstitions have grown up around the tradition of saints' relics, remembering our origins as a church is, when properly understood, a very moving and inspiring custom of the church.

For whatever reason, the tradition of patron saints reminds us of those who have gone before us, walking the path we are also called to walk. The notion of patronage links the present community to the charism or charisms of the particular saint who serves as a special guardian and supporter of the community. For example, St. Louis the King was especially dedicated to the poor of his kingdom. Though all Christians are called to have a special concern for the poor, those who belong to communities under the patronage of St. Louis have a special charge to reach out to the poor in service and love. Through the diffusive character and continuing relevance of the saints in the life of the church, the community of faith is constantly being schooled in the ways of discipleship and the gospel life we are each called to live. By remembering saints through the tradition of patronage or through the celebration of saints' feast days, the church reminds us of those still in our midst, even if in a veiled way, holding them up to us as examples of faith-filled discipleship.

Saints as Role Models of Faith and Love

Arguably the most important function of a saint is their role as an exemplar of the Christian life for the believing community. More than creeds, humans need people to believe in. It might well be that no one understood this better than God who chose to become a human person to save us. It is not a law engraved on stone but a living person through whom God saves. But, it is a piece of simple human wisdom that words are cheap. Though such wisdom makes the skin of every writer and English teacher crawl, the point is that in human interaction it is easy to make statements but it is tremendously difficult to enact behaviors. It is easy to profess undying love but it is the challenge of a lifetime to live up to that profession each and every day. It is easy to speak of our honesty and integrity but being honest and embodying our integrity each day can be a monumental struggle. It is easy to profess belief in God but another thing entirely to allow our lives to be shaped by that belief. That is why we have a tendency to admire people who are willing and able to put their words into concrete practice each day.

In James Carroll's classic novel *Prince of Peace*, when one of the primary characters ponders how to eulogize his oldest and dearest friend, he thinks back on his friend Michael Maguire's work as a priest and as an anti-Viet Nam War protester. He believes Michael was "the flower of Catholic life, the best we had, the one who went before us and showed that it was safe."[4] The saints may not show us that living the Christian life is safe, but perhaps more importantly they went before us to show that it was possible. On the surface, the teaching of Jesus encountered in the gospel tradition seems impossible to fulfill. In an age of global terrorism, how can one turn the other cheek? Each week, the news is filled with stories of suicide attacks, mass killings, and gun battles inspired by the fanaticism and ignorance of foreign or domestic terrorists. Shopping malls, movie theaters, schools, college campuses, concert venues, company holiday parties, night clubs, churches, and numerous other locations are no longer places where people can gather to enjoy a few moments of peace and good will in their lives.

---

4. Carroll, *Prince of Peace*, 550.

Part IV: Saints

Now those locations are targets for the warped minds of terrorists and the homicidal and suicidal among us. How does one turn the other cheek as Jesus taught?[5]

Like God commanding Abraham to sacrifice Isaac, some of what Jesus says strikes us as unreasonable and at times even inhuman. For example, when a man approaches Jesus to assure him he will follow the Lord as soon as he buries his father, Jesus replies, "Let the dead bury their own dead; but as for you, go and proclaim the Kingdom of God."[6] In response to the rich young man's question about entrance into eternal life, Jesus counsels him that he must sell everything he owns, give it to the poor, then follow Jesus.[7] In a world where people kill the innocent to advance their cause, Jesus calls us to love our enemies.[8] To turn another of Jesus' sayings on its head,[9] it is challenging sometimes to love those who love you. How much more challenging to love those who seek to destroy you? How do you fulfill the role of the blessed peacemaker when confronting an enemy with whom discourse is not possible? Our culture rewards those who hunger and thirst to get ahead not those who seek justice. Those Jesus considers blessed are those who often inhabit a way of life our culture often actively encourages us to avoid.[10]

Of course, interpreting the moral teaching of Jesus is a complex affair and the implementation of his teaching is indeed complicated. But, on the surface, it can be disheartening when disciples believe they are leading a good life but seem to come up far short when evaluating their lives against the standards Jesus establishes in the gospels. We can often seek to avoid the demands of the gospel by assuring ourselves that such a life was easy for Jesus. After all, he was divine and did not share in the struggles and uncertainties we face each day. He could even accept his death on the cross because he knew about the resurrection in advance. (In fairness, thanks to his resurrection, I could argue we have a clearer view of the future than he possessed at the time of his death.) His unique status made everything easier for him. It is the same logic we often apply to saints by an exaggerated focus on the mysterious and mystical. The distance we create between

5. Matt. 5:38-42.
6. Luke 9:59-60.
7. Mark 10:17-22.
8. Matt. 5:43-48.
9. Matt. 5:46-48.
10. Matt. 5:3-12.

saints and ourselves provides us with a built-in justification for why they responded to God's call with such generosity and courage and why we are so often hesitant to do so.

The chasm we create often undermines the greatest gift the saints offer to the church in every age, the witness of their example. Like Michael Maguire, they went before us to show us we could live the gospel life because they did. They had all the same doubts and uncertainties, failings and foibles we possess. Living a life of faith has never been easy, no matter what century you live in. There has never been a time when God's call was clearer or when God's expectations were easier to meet. The specific details of the challenges faced by each era may be different but the reality of those difficult challenges remains. What the example of the saints' lives reminds us is that, though it is never easy to respond to God's call and though we may never have absolute certainty about the substance of that call, it is always possible to respond within the bounds of our own time and place. We need only pray for the grace necessary to do so and possess the courage to commit despite the challenges and struggles we face. In that regard, the saints stand as constant reminders that humans are capable, when surrendering to God's grace, of being faithful to the gospel summons to proclaim the kingdom of God in word and deed. We cannot claim it is an impossible task because we know they did it despite their weaknesses and limitations and the challenges of their times. God's grace did not remove their shortcomings or make them perfect. But, they were open enough to the promptings of the Holy Spirit to give their lives in service to the gospel. They call out to us across the centuries to be open enough and let God do some pretty great things through us.

Mary as Saint

Arguably the most popular of the Catholic saints is Mary the Mother of God. But, it is important to understand why Mary is rightly regarded as one of the foremost saints in the church. Through Mary we can appreciate this dimension of the ongoing significance of the saints in the life of the church. In Luke's gospel, Jesus is portrayed as responding to a woman who calls out from the crowd, "Blessed is the womb that carried you and the breasts at which you nursed." Jesus responds, "Rather, blessed are those who hear the word of God and observe it."[11] As a young boy, I remember struggling with

11. Luke 11:27-28.

this reading, believing Jesus was disrespecting his mother by his answer. As I grew, I began to realize that far from disrespecting his mother, Jesus was praising her. Jesus tries to focus our praise of Mary on the right reason. Mary's blessedness resides not simply in the fact that she bore and raised him. What makes Mary truly blessed is that she heard the word of God and observed it. Earlier in Luke's gospel we read Mary's response to the news shared with her by the angel Gabriel, "Behold, I am the handmaid of the Lord. May it be done to me according to your word."[12] When confronted with the very first presentation of the good news, Mary offers her fiat, her yes to God. When visiting Elizabeth, her kinswoman declares, "And blessed is she who believed that there would be a fulfillment of what was spoken to her by the Lord."[13] Particularly for the author of the Gospel of Luke, Mary is the first disciple of her son Jesus.

To be sure, a cult has grown up around Mary that has experienced some risky excesses. Many Catholics themselves participate in practices or speak of Mary in ways that are both out of step with the teaching of the church and that diminish her significance as a role model for discipleship. This often leads to confusion among our sisters and brothers in Protestant communities. For example, many Catholics will state that they pray to Mary. This is not the teaching of the church. As we stated earlier, prayer is primarily directed to God or Jesus and the Holy Spirit. We may ask Mary to pray with us in the same way we ask other saints, discussed earlier in the chapter, to pray for us. But, we do not pray to Mary. Resulting from some of the exalted titles we give to Mary, e.g. Queen of Heaven, many mistakenly believe Mary had a necessary role in Christ's act of redemption. Some have even suggested the title Co-Redemptrix should be applied to Mary. Unfortunately, such claims only further to muddy the waters of the Christian community's understanding of the significance of Mary. To be sure, Mary had a unique and special role in salvation history, being called by God to be the mother of his Son. But, she remains, like the rest of us, a human being in need of the saving grace offered through Jesus her Son. Even when the church declared Mary 'theotokos,' or Mother of God, the title had less to do with Mary than with the church's claims about Jesus. If the church was correct in proclaiming Jesus to be fully divine and Mary was his mother than she must be the Mother of God. To suggest otherwise would be to diminish the church's claims about the divinity of her son Jesus.

12. Luke 1:38.
13. Luke 1:45.

The church's beliefs about the saints apply equally to Mary. She continues to be a member of the believing community. As such, we can continue to ask her to pray for and with us to God. In fact, the tradition points to Mary's intercession at the wedding feast in Cana as a biblical template for saints' ongoing ability to intercede with Jesus on our behalf. She continues to serve the believing community as a role model of fidelity, courage, generosity, and perseverance. Many Catholics have a special devotion to Mary because of her great faith, her closeness to Jesus, and the love she has for the church. Despite her faith, she suffered greatly, including and most painfully, the loss of her son. Her humanity moves many believers to embody faith, hope, and love in their own lives and in the midst of their own struggles. However, such a devotion is not a requirement of Catholic faith. For some, they may feel a special closeness to St. Francis or St. Anthony, St. Dominic or St. Ignatius Loyola. For others, they may feel a unique bond with St. Teresa of Avila or Catherine of Sienna, St. Claire or Mary, the Mother of God. Still others may not feel a particular bond with any of the saints. Regardless, the saints remain members of the faith community. Therefore, we can have an ongoing relationship with them, we can talk with them, and we can ask them to pray for us or for a particular need the way we often unthinkingly do with family, friends, and fellow believers. And perhaps most important, we can look to them for guidance, for inspiration, and for hope, knowing that despite their personal limitations and the limitations of the times in which they lived, they show us that it is possible to respond to the call of God with generosity, courage, and love. What is required of us is what was required of Mary, to hear the word of God, obey it, and believe that the word the Lord speaks will be fulfilled.

Part V

Structure

*How Does Your Church Organize and
Operate Local Congregations?*

Chapter 9

Of Institutions and Kingdoms
The Structure of the Church

LYLE K. WEISS

Values and Institutions

IN HIS BOOK 'THE Quartet: Orchestrating the Second American Revolution, 1783-1789' the distinguished scholar of the American Revolution and the founding of the nation, Joseph J. Ellis, describes in detail the context within which the American Constitution was born.[1] Of primary concern to, among others, the quartet of James Madison, John Jay, Alexander Hamilton, and George Washington, was the fear that the Articles of Confederation were unsuitable for the establishment of an American nation. Under the weak articles, they envisioned a collapse of the harmony that existed among the colonies in the battle for independence. This fear anticipated a splitting of the colonies into thirteen sovereign nations or a number of regional confederacies, either of which would represent the death knell of the nation that the fight for independence had made possible. It was the hope of this quartet of political thinkers, philosophers, lawyers, and leaders, that the constitution would enshrine in structure and substance the implications of Jefferson's Declaration of Independence that articulated the spirit of the American Revolution. Without the appropriate structures, structures faithful to the guiding impulses of the revolutionary spirit, the enterprise would

---

1. Ellis, *The Quartet*.

PART V: STRUCTURE

fail. With the appropriate structures, that revolutionary spirit would find enduring expression in the life of a people and nation.

To be human is to be an actor on the stage of history. As embodied spirits, our beliefs, fears, values, and struggles find concrete expression on that historical stage. We may not all have our names or deeds included on the pages of history books, but everything we do finds expression within the parameters of time and space. What the quartet of founding American fathers understood was that the ideas and values, passions and vision of the founding generation would be for naught if they did not find expression in concrete experience. In this particular circumstance, they needed to devise a system of government that would embody the ideals and values that had united the colonies in their drive for independence and would make of them the nation first glimpsed in that concerted effort to be free. Without such a government, those ideals and values would find themselves played out, relegated to the dustbin of history as pie in the sky thinking without the genuine hope of ever being realized. Nearly two centuries later, when speaking of the legacy of his brother John, Bobby Kennedy in his Day of Affirmation Address at the University of Capetown in June, 1966, stated that his brother had shared with the world his "belief that idealism, high aspiration and deep convictions are not incompatible with the most practical and efficient of programs." It was a sentiment with which the founders would have agreed, believing as they did that the high ideals and deep convictions of the movement for independence could find lasting expression in the structures of a government strong enough to transform the confederacy into a united nation.

That drive to institutionalize the revolutionary impulses of the founding generation is also true in the experience of the Christian community. Many theologians and scholars argue that Jesus believed his speedy return and the fulfillment of God's promises would come within the lifetime of his earliest disciples.[2] If you expect the end of the world to occur next week, you really do not need to waste time on retirement savings. But, if you do not know when the end is to occur, you need to put in place the systems and structures necessary to care for you and your family during your twilight years. Like the American Spirit of '76, Jesus' proclamation of the kingdom of God unleashed a revolutionary zeal resulting in the spread of what was originally called the Way to the farthest reaches of the known world. But, as time passed, it became increasingly clear to the leaders of the

---

2. Matt. 16:27-28; Mark 14:61-62.

Jesus Movement that it was necessary to develop systems and structures that would shape and guide the community as it walked on pilgrimage until the day when the Lord would return. Those systems and structures would necessarily be shaped by the context of the successive ages through which the church and the human family as a whole passed. Whether that influence was good or bad, and it has definitely been both, the best leaders and thinkers in the church confronted the challenge in each age to enshrine the values, virtues, and principles of the kingdom Jesus proclaimed in concrete structures and systems of governance and leadership. It is true that the church has made some wrong turns over the course of its 2000-year history, that it has suffered at times under the burden of poor leadership, and that it has paid too much or too little attention to the shaping influence of the world around it. As the Sulpician theologian Fred Cwiekowski has written, considering the church's acceptance of various institutional features it borrowed from the world around it as it developed in its early life, "On the positive side, the Christian Church became organizationally a powerful vehicle for evangelization. However, the negative side meant an uncritical acceptance of some organizational structures and styles which at times sadly hindered the witness and mission of the church."[3] Despite this acceptance referenced by Cwiekowski, which reflects a continuing struggle in the life of the church regarding its relationship to the larger world, it should not delegitimize the fundamental pursuit of embodying the spirit and substance of the life, death, and resurrection of Jesus and the ongoing presence and inspiration of the Holy Spirit in the way the church is structured and shaped.

In this chapter we will be examining the contemporary embodiment of that pursuit, understanding that the current result has been shaped over the course of 2,000 years and will continue to be shaped as the church moves through history. First, we will look at why there is a church at all. We live in a time in which many believe in God but do not feel it necessary to have any connection with institutionalized religion. For this reason, it is important to at least outline the necessity of the church. Second, we will examine ways to think about the church. Too often, the Roman Catholic Church is reduced to a hierarchical institution. But, to engage in such reduction is to miss the depth and breadth of the church's identity and mission. And lastly, we will make some more basic and practical observations about the structure and operation of the church today.

3. Cwiekowski, S.S., *The Beginnings of the Church*, 188.

PART V: STRUCTURE

The Necessity of the Institutional Church

The late great Sulpician biblical scholar, Raymond E. Brown, wrote, correctly, that the genealogy opening Matthew's gospel is less a matter of historical record than theological vision.[4] Jesus' ancestors are grouped into three sections of 14 despite the fact that the three timeframes represent vastly different periods of time. The purpose of the genealogy is to ground the story Matthew is about to relate in the narrative of ancient Israel. The first group of 14[5] includes the names of the patriarchs, names both familiar and significant. Imagine if one were grounding the story of a contemporary American figure in the narrative of the nation's history, the first group would include the names of Washington, Jefferson, Adams, and Franklin. Americans know these names and, with varying degrees of detail, are aware that these men are the large characters who together helped to found the nation. The author of Matthew's gospel wants his audience to know that the story of Jesus flows from the very foundation of the people and nation.

The third group[6] consists of names of people who have been lost to history, of anonymous people who fill the world's cemeteries. Other than their appearance in this list, their names make no imprint upon the pages of history. For the author of Matthew, this grouping is an expression of his deep respect for those nameless faces throughout history who, in every generation, quietly live out their faith, keeping the promise of the good news alive and making the faith real for the generations to follow. This grouping represents those of us whose names will never darken the historical record but through whom the faith is passed forward from generation to generation and the link to all that came before is maintained and deepened. History books are often written to memorialize the generals who plan and command or presidents and kings who lead. But, beyond the names of the famous are the countless nameless soldiers and citizens following those orders and making their own contributions to society who steer the course of history. The genealogy of Matthew understands the necessary contributions of the founding fathers, the patriarchs, but it also recognizes the promise inherent in that contribution can never be fulfilled without the persistent fidelity of the many whom history will never remember.

---

4. See Brown, *The Birth of the Messiah* and *A Coming Christ in Advent*, 16-26.
5. Matt. 1:2-6.
6. Matt. 1:12-16.

The second group of 14,[7] given our focus for this chapter, is more like the first group. It too includes names extremely familiar and significant to the ancient community. Representing the period of the monarchy, the names of David, Solomon, Rehoboam, Hezekiah, and Josiah populate this group recalling for the ancient community the lives and contributions of the kings of past ages. Again, for an American, it would be like having a genealogy that, after the names of the founders, included the names of Presidents Lincoln, Roosevelt, Kennedy, Eisenhower, Wilson, and Reagan. In fact, it was during the period of the monarchy, amidst its successes and failures, that the notion of a future messiah had its origins. David expanded the boundaries and influence of the kingdom through conquest after which he reigned over a period of peace and prosperity that the ancient Israelites, from the often desperate and devastating experiences they suffered, looked back on with longing. They began to understand that God would act in dramatic fashion at some point in the future when a messiah, an anointed of God from the line of David, would come and reestablish forever the age of God's peace and prosperity.

The author of the Gospel of Matthew understood that the elements critical to, and present in, the story leading up to the coming of the messiah would also be present in the aftermath of the messiah's advent. The promise to Abraham that Israel would be the source of blessing for all the nations would find its fulfillment in the preaching of the good news to the ends of the earth, the call to the followers of Jesus to make disciples of all nations, a call the church inherits in each successive age. The nameless men and women who kept the faith alive, especially in dark times, would have their counterparts in the Christian community in the many who, though never appearing in the history books, would become heralds of the good news in every age. And of course, important for our purposes, the institution of the monarchy that played such an important role in the narrative leading to the expectation of the messiah, would have its counterpart in the institution of the church that would proclaim the good news of that messiah to the ends of the earth. More than any other gospel, Matthew emphasizes the centrality of the church. For the author of Matthew's gospel, those who envision the followers of Jesus existing without an institutional expression do not understand the story that led to the coming of the messiah nor do they understand the story of the community that was to flow from the messiah's life, death, and resurrection.

---

7. Matt. 1:6b-11.

Part V: Structure

Like the founders of the American form of government, the question for the early believers was not whether there should be an institutional expression of the originating impulses and values which established the community. The question was what kind of institution can be created that will reflect and embody the kingdom Jesus proclaimed and for which he died and was raised. Admittedly, based upon the New Testament evidence, church structure during the New Testament period was quite diverse. That those expressions were different is not, from one perspective, the most significant point. That some were more charismatic in nature and some more hierarchical in nature affirms the early efforts to establish communities that looked, sounded, and felt like the messiah who had called them into being. The broader and more important point to consider here is that the earliest believers and earliest communities recognized the necessity of the church community as it moved through history proclaiming the gospel and carrying on the mission of Jesus. In our day, the religious category experiencing the largest growth consists of those believers who identify themselves as spiritual but not religious. They come in various shapes and sizes but seem to share the view that spirituality is an individual experience and that institutional forms of religion inhibit the freedom of believers to experience the presence of God. This mentality exists awkwardly alongside the biblical vision which is decidedly corporate in nature. For the ancient Jews, God calls a people, a Qahal, not a collection of unrelated individuals. For Matthew especially but for the other New Testament authors as well, God calls believers into communion. To reduce the gospel to a series of ethical teachings or spiritual practices by which one intends to live without inclusion and participation in the institution of the church risks missing an important and necessary element in the substance of the gospel.

This is a crucial element in the proclamation of the gospel, particularly in our world today in which we seem to be involved in Hobbes' war of all against each. Though God's call is deeply personal, it is never private. Rather, from the beginning, God called a people to be his own and to serve as the means by and through which the nations of the world would be blessed. God called a people, a call that found expression in the corporate life of that people through the centuries. For Christians, the gospel calls us to live in Jesus through the Spirit together, belonging to the institution flowing from and striving to embody in the world the life, death, and resurrection of the messiah. Images of the church, for example the body of Christ and the people of God, affirm this corporate, communitarian vision. Of course, affirming the necessity and importance of the church does not deny or reject any and all legitimate calls for the church to be a more faithful witness to the gospel in the world or for more specific changes and reforms when they are needed. It is, however, to affirm the necessity of the community in an age when self-interest challenges the notion of community as a significant and necessary value.

Structure of the Church

The question that gives this chapter its focus involves how the church is organized and how it operates. For the Roman Catholic Church, this question has global implications given the organizational principles that inform the church's shape at both the macro and micro levels. It is important to consider this question from a broader perspective particularly concerning the Roman Catholic approach because it is too often the hierarchical structure of the church that is at issue behind many of the debates that make their way into newspaper and magazine headlines. Although it is true that the church functions as a hierarchical institution, it is important to clarify at the outset that to fully understand the nature and mission of the church requires a willingness to accept that the church is more than a hierarchically structured institution. In fact, the hierarchical framework of the church may be the least important approach to understanding the identity and mission of the church.

In his important work "Models of the Church,"[8] the theologian Avery Cardinal Dulles identified six ways of understanding the identity and mission of the church, six ways that exert influence on the shape, structure, and self-awareness of the church: church as mystical communion, church as community of disciples, church as sacrament, church as herald, church as servant, and church as institution. It is true that the church as an institution is rightly included among the models articulated by Cardinal Dulles. But, it is equally important to recognize it is not the only, or most important, model. In fact, none of the models he identifies can stand alone. Dulles insists that it is vitally necessary that we see the necessity and validity of all models for forming a broader, more substantial understanding of what it means to be the church. Often, problems in the church have stemmed from an unwillingness to include, or an ignorance about, the necessity of all the models, instead reducing the vision of the church to only one or perhaps

8. Dulles, *Models of the Church*.

two at any given time. To appreciate the structure of the church requires that we understand that the church is in fact a hierarchically organized institution but that it is also a mystical communion with the blessed Trinity, a sacrament in the world of God's presence and love, a herald of the good news of what God has done in Jesus through the Holy Spirit, a servant of the community and world, and a community of equal disciples following in the footsteps of Jesus, a later edition in Dulles' own thought and experience. In other words, the church is more than priests, bishops, cardinals, and popes. Embracing each of the models allows for a more balanced, nuanced, and robust understanding of the church's identity and mission and of the contributions we are each called upon to make to the work of the church.

During my days in the seminary, I remember hearing a story told about a bishop who believed the most important date that should appear on his grave marker was not the date of his birth, the date of his ordination to the priesthood, or the day he was ordained a bishop. For this bishop, the most important date was that of his baptism. The Second Vatican Council's Dogmatic Constitution on the Church, Lumen Gentium, articulated the notion that all Christians are called to holiness of life. "It is therefore quite clear that all Christians in any state or walk of life are called to the fullness of Christian life and to the perfection of love, and by this holiness a more human manner of life is fostered also in earthly society."[9] All members of the Christian community, regardless of title, authority, or role, are called to holiness. It is this universal call to holiness that is extended to each of us in baptism. For this reason, the previously mentioned bishop saw baptism as the most important date because he believed it is the universal call to holiness that is most significant for believers rather than the specific path they follow in its pursuit.

To speak of the structure of the church in light of the universal call to holiness is to affirm the role each believer plays in the church's mission to proclaim and embody the kingdom of God. Too often, discussions of church structure operate from the hierarchical, pyramidal vision with the pope at the top, followed by cardinals, archbishops, bishops, priests, deacons, religious, and laity. Such a view limits an understanding of the church to structures of authority and governance. Recalling our earlier reflections on Dulles' models of the church, each model would envision the structure of the church differently. The institutional model obviously places its emphasis on the hierarchical ordering of leadership in the church. Other

---

9. Lumen Gentium, 40.

models, which understand that all believers as a result of baptism and the universal call to holiness are commissioned to proclaim the gospel in word and deed, place emphasis less on structures of authority and more on the task of living and proclaiming the good news both within the community and throughout the larger world.

It is worth noting that the universal call to holiness and the shared responsibility of proclaiming the gospel present in most of Dulles' models understand the laity to possess a profound and crucial mission. Sadly, in our day the term laity is generally used to refer to the ignorance of the person involved. When dealing with a tricky legal issue, we might ask the lawyer to explain it in laymen's terms. An expert might chide us by suggesting we could never understand because we are just laymen. We may, in an act of self-deprecation, suggest that we are 'just layman' when confronting a particular question. Our use of the term betrays our acceptance of our place in the hierarchical pecking order. Pope Pius X, in his encyclical *Vehementer Nos*, speaks of the church as an unequal society with two different types of categories of persons, the pastors and the flock. In this view the flock have no responsibility other than "the duty but to allow itself to be led and to follow its pastors as a docile flock."[10] This view is an official articulation of the laity as called to pray, pay, and obey so popular in the decades leading up to the Second Vatican Council and still all too alive in certain communities. Of course, it is true that there is tremendous disparity among the clergy and laity regarding familiarity with the theological tradition of the church. But, we must never let this more popular use of the term laity undermine an understanding and appreciation of the fact that the laity, derived from their baptism and the universal call to holiness, have a profound mission to spread the gospel in their families, communities, and the larger world. Increasingly, many members of the lay faithful are exercising leadership in parish and diocesan ministries and many are pursuing and obtaining graduate and doctoral degrees, passing on the theological tradition of the church to the next generation through classroom instruction, public lectures, and books and articles. But, regardless of whether one is a lay theologian or a parish minister, or if one is a lawyer, a novelist, a food service professional, or a tax accountant, all the laity share in the fundamental mission of the church to proclaim the gospel in every age and to be a leaven in society for the building up of God's kingdom.

---

10. Pius X, *Vehementer Nos*, 1906.

Part V: Structure

Perhaps the most powerful language used to articulate the Roman Catholic Church's understanding of its structure is that of communion. In the Gospel of John, on the night before he died, Jesus prayed that all his disciples might be one.[11] This prayer of Jesus has found expression in the church's desire through the centuries to maintain communion among the various local churches through common belief, common practice, and common structure under the leadership of the pope and the college of bishops. As the original generation of apostles began dying off and as examples of false teachers and false teaching began to spread, e.g. Gnosticism, (the notion of private revelation given to only a select few), the earliest communities became increasingly concerned about protecting and preserving the deposit of faith.[12] One dimension of this protection and preservation involved the necessity of communion between churches. This communion was affirmed through the shared teachings of these wide-ranging communities. Those who were teaching a similar vision of the gospel were in communion with each other.[13]

To be sure, the notion of communion developed over a period of centuries even as it continues to develop today. The communion existing between local churches and the universal church remains in part based upon fundamental creedal statements, the shared vision of the gospel that finds expression in a body of teaching and practices, and the celebration of the sacraments. The notion of communion has its origin in the experience of the early church. That experience affirmed the need for combatting what was false and affirming what was commonly held and practiced. Such combat and affirmation remain today. It would be mistaken, however, for us to think that Peter was touring the world to shouts of Holy Father while wearing white escorted by his fellow apostles in their cardinal red or magenta trimmed cassocks, trailed no doubt by Swiss Guards and riding in a pope-mobile pulled by a donkey. I mention this not to offend but to affirm for contemporary believers that the church as we now know it has not always existed in its current shape and form. The church has been shaped by the context of the times through which it has passed, borrowing and applying the structures of the day to church organization and governance with decidedly mixed results. Societal systems down through the centuries with monarchs and princes often provided easy mingling with the

---

11. John 17:11.
12. 1 Tim. 6:20; 2 Tim. 1:12, 14.
13. McBrien, 42ff.

necessity for leadership in the church. As the church has moved through history, encountering various systems, philosophies, and perspectives, we have inherited a community organized by principles and norms that were not mandated by Jesus from the beginning but adopted by the church as it sought in every age to symbolize and embody the kingdom of God in its institutional life. Reminding ourselves that the church did not descend from heaven in its current form can free us to think through in each generation the need to structure the church in a way that best reflects and embodies the values of the gospel.

Current Structure

It is beyond the scope of this chapter to examine the historical unfolding of the structure of the church from the earliest communities to the highly organized and systematized form of today. Evaluating that development and the church's current form involve other theological debates that impinge upon such an evaluation. For example, as mentioned in an earlier chapter, there are many in the church who still maintain the belief that Jesus intended to found a new religion and therefore interpret his actions in light of that intention. When viewed from within this context, the Last Supper is an ordination ritual and the disciples are the first priests and bishops of the church. However, as we saw, others in the church reject this view. This group embraces instead the claim that Jesus did not intend to found a new religion. Rather, his intention was to reform Judaism. The Last Supper then is not an effort to organize the new religion and establish fundamental policies of that new religion but a final shared meal which he hoped would call to mind for his followers his mission and his death. Depending upon your answer to the question of whether Jesus intended to found a new religion, you will develop differing interpretations to the same texts of sacred scripture and understand the development of the church in its institutional form quite differently. In modern times, prior to the Second Vatican Council, the church's understanding of itself and the justification of its institutional structures was grounded in its belief that Jesus did intend to found a new religion and supported the biblical interpretations flowing from that fundamental belief. Critics maintain, rightly, that critical contemporary elements of church identity and structure were not in place during the New Testament period and, therefore, developed over centuries. Even if both sides agreed with such a claim, the question would still be hotly debated whether

PART V: STRUCTURE

that development was always Spirit inspired or flowed from an uncritical acceptance as Cwiekoswki suggested earlier.

For our purposes, we shall have to leave this discussion and instead focus our attention on the organizational structure of the church as it currently exists and as believers currently experience it rather than as some critics might claim it should be, always recalling that the organizational structure of the church is but a fraction of what the church is and should always aspire to be. As helpful and as necessary as these ongoing theological debates are, it is nevertheless the focus of this chapter that we explain the way the church is currently structured, how it operates, and the reasons offered in support of such structure and operation so that members of the Roman Catholic Church and other interested believers might understand the current structure and how it functions. How is leadership structured in the church and how do local churches relate to and with each other? Given the central importance of the sacraments in Catholic theology and life, the structure of the church as most believers experience it is shaped by the notion of priesthood and its service to the believing community.

Each local parish operates within the power structure established by the broader hierarchical structure of the universal church. The pastor is a priest who has been ordained by the bishop to support the pastoral ministry and leadership of the bishop who is both the head of the local church and the symbol of its communion with the universal church. The parish ministers of the local church serve under the authority of the pastor who serves under the authority of the local bishop. All of the parishes within a designated region, called a diocese, operate under the authority of the local bishop. The word diocese comes from a Greek word meaning administration and is used to refer to a territory under the administrative leadership of the local bishop. An archdiocese is the head diocese of an ecclesiastical, or church, province. An archdiocese, which is also called a metropolitan see, consists of itself and the subordinate dioceses assigned to it. A diocese is headed by a bishop whereas an archdiocese is headed by an archbishop. The archdiocese may be granted the title due to its size or historical importance. For example, the Archdiocese of Baltimore is not very significant from the perspective of the size of its Catholic population. However, it has tremendous historical importance as the original, or primatial, see in the United States.

Some priests may also possess the title of monsignor. This title signifies a priest who has been given the title by the pope for his distinguished service to the church. In the English-speaking world, the title monsignor refers to priests who have been so designated. But, they remain members of the presbyterate without duties necessarily different from other priests. However, in various parts of the non-English speaking world, the form of address of monsignor may refer to a bishop. For readers who may have seen the film "Romero,"[14] about the assassinated Archbishop of San Salvador (and if you have not seen it, I highly recommend it), he is referred to as Monsenor Romero. In English-speaking countries, monsignors are not bishops. At the local parish, priests exercise administrative and sacramental authority over the community. Though other priests and lay ministers may support him in the pastoral ministry of the local church, for example pastoral councils and finance committees, their work flows from his authority as the pastor. His authority flows from the authority of the local bishop in who's pastoral ministry the priest shares. Each of the local churches are in communion with each other through their share in the ministry of the bishop.

The structure of the universal church shapes the structure of the church at the local level. The pope, in communion with the college of bishops spread throughout the world, exercises supreme leadership, pastoral ministry, and authority in the church. An important teaching in the Roman Catholic tradition regarding structure is the notion of apostolic succession. Apostolic succession refers to the belief that Jesus named the Twelve the first apostles. They then named their successors, the bishops, and so on down the line to the present day. It is the Roman Catholic Church's claim that it alone can trace its roots back to the first apostles. The pope is the successor of St. Peter and exercises his primacy in the church. The teaching suggests that as Peter was primary among the apostles, so too is the pope primary among the bishops. He is the first among equals. The bishops are the descendants of the apostles, tracing their identity and authority back to the first apostles. It was through the bishops that the deposit of faith was passed down from generation to generation. Therefore, the bishops are the embodiment and the sign of unity among the churches, continuing to be the instrument of the protection and preservation of the deposit of faith in every age.

---

14. *Romero*, Paulist Pictures, 1989.

Part V: Structure

Conclusion

The identity, self-understanding, and mission of the church are far too broad to be reduced to any one image or model. The Church is conceived of as the people of God, the body of Christ, and the temple of the Holy Spirit, among other images and symbols. To speak of the church as an institution is to capture only a fraction of who and what the church is and is called to be. To return to our use of analogies from the experience of the United States, it would be hopelessly and wrongheadedly reductive to think of the identity and mission of our nation as concerned only with our political leaders. When earlier speaking of the genealogy in Matthew's gospel, we noted that the first group consisted of the founders, the second group consisted of the monarchy, and the third group consisted of the nameless people from history. The promise God entered into with the patriarchs was often violated by the monarchs of Israel. It was the nameless people of history who kept the promise alive and carried it forward, linking the promise to the advent of the messiah. To reduce the church simply to a discussion of the actions and pronouncements of popes, bishops, and priests would be to misunderstand who and what the church is and why it exists. To understand more appropriately what the church is and why it exists requires equal attention paid to the various models articulated by Avery Dulles and expounded upon by others since. But, we remain a hierarchically organized institution striving to embody in our structures and governance the principles and values of the kingdom Jesus proclaimed and for which he died. We must always be vigilant that we only maintain forms of governance and authority that embody the gospel. Such vigilance is one of the many crucial responsibilities of the church in every age. The beliefs we teach, the sacramental celebrations we perform, the actions on behalf of justice and peace we pursue, and the way we organize ourselves are all dimensions of our one proclamation of the gospel. Only through such vigilance and acceptance of the church as an unfinished community moving through history will we continue to grow and develop, becoming a greater reflection in history of our crucified and risen Lord.

Chapter 10

Presbyterianism

Representative Church Government

Thomas M. Tasselmyer

The Birth of the Church

As a devout Jew, "church" for Jesus was Saturday in the synagogue to hear psalms, a reading from Scripture, a sermon, and prayers. And, after He ascended into heaven forty days following His resurrection, the disciples continued to worship in the same way, gathering at synagogues and at the temple in Jerusalem as devout Jews organized in a sect they called "The Way." However, even as they observed the Jewish laws and rituals, under the leadership of the apostles they began to recognize the death and resurrection of Jesus, and the coming of the Holy Spirit on Pentecost, as divine events that had produced in them a unique gathering of God's people. Like the covenant people of God who were called out to the desert wilderness, the disciples of Jesus saw themselves as an *ekklesia*, the Greek word meaning an assembly of "called out ones," translated in English as "church."

The infant *ekklesia*, or church, united around the teaching of the apostles and the two ceremonies that recalled the death and resurrection of Jesus and the coming of the Spirit: baptism and the Lord's Supper. The young church grew rapidly, and the growth created tension among the various people it attracted, and the people with whom it interacted. Many Greek-speaking Hellenist Jews, for example, who came to Jerusalem from outside of Palestine joined the church and created internal tension between Hebraic Jews and Grecian Jews. Preaching Jesus as the long-awaited, but now crucified Messiah, the church sparked violent opposition from traditional Jewish authorities who were waiting for a militant, triumphant Messiah to free them from Rome.

Around the year 36 CE, a member of the church named Stephen who was "full of God's grace and power" preached a sermon about Jesus as the crucified Messiah and was stoned to death for blasphemy.[1] The death of Stephen sent Hellenist Jews in the Jerusalem church fleeing for their lives, effectively turning the church into a missionary movement. Some of the refugees went to Antioch in Syria where, for the first time, Gentiles were evangelized and opponents of the followers of Jesus were called the supposedly derogatory name: "Christians."

One of those chasing the followers of Jesus out of the Jerusalem synagogues was a man named Saul of Tarsus. Saul was there watching as Stephen was martyred. Then, on his way to Damascus to root out more followers of Jesus, Saul was confronted by the risen Jesus Himself. With a blinding flash of light, Saul was knocked to the ground, stopped in his tracks, and commissioned by Jesus as an apostle to preach the gospel to the Gentiles.[2] Saul took the Greek-friendly name Paul, and with the same zeal he once used to persecute Christians, channeled his energy into evangelizing pagans in Greece, Asia Minor, and eventually, Rome. His efforts were so effective, by the end of the first century the church was predominantly Gentile, not Jewish.

Paul, the once ultra-legalist Pharisee, was teaching the Gentiles that Christianity does not require observance of the Law of Moses; righteousness comes by the grace of God through faith in Jesus Christ. But Paul's good news meant those who converted held beliefs that were outside of what established Jewish communities required, making it necessary for Paul to create new Christian communities. In each of the cities where he preached the gospel, Paul had to plant a church.

Paul tells us that what he preached was based on a super-natural revelation from Jesus: ". . . the gospel I preached is not of human origin. I did not receive it from any man, nor was I taught it; rather, I received it by revelation from Jesus Christ."[3] Likewise, his understanding of how to

---

1. Acts 6-7.
2. Acts 9.
3. Galatians 1:11-12.

celebrate the Lord's Supper,[4] his instructions for struggling marriages,[5] and his teaching that preachers of the gospel should be paid,[6] were all based on what was revealed to him by Jesus Christ. So, it seems safe to assume that the churches Paul started were organized with the teachings of Jesus in mind; the principles guiding the formation of the earliest visible church came from Christ.

A Primitive Ecclesiology

Unfortunately, the Gospel writers recorded very little from the mouth of Jesus himself about the structure and day-to-day operation of the church. In fact, only in the Gospel of Matthew do we hear Jesus specifically mention the church. One particularly insightful exchange, however, is recorded by Matthew after the apostle Peter aces Jesus's one-question pop quiz, "Who do you say I am?"[7] Peter answered Jesus by saying, "You are the Messiah, the Son of the living God."[8] Then Jesus commended him with the reply, "Blessed are you, Simon son of Jonah, for this was not revealed to you by flesh and blood, but by my Father in heaven. And I tell you that you are Peter, and on this rock I will build my church, and the gates of Hades will not overcome it. I will give you the keys of the kingdom of heaven; whatever you bind on earth will be bound in heaven, and whatever you loose on earth will be loosed in heaven."[9] In this passage we get a picture of what Jesus considers to be some fundamental principles regarding the structure and operation of the church.

First, we see that when Peter states his belief in Jesus as the Messiah, Jesus announces that Peter's belief is a blessing and a gift from God, and then He immediately begins to elaborate on the building up of His church. Peter's belief makes evident the church, which is composed of those who, like Peter, receive the gift of belief. These are God's elect; the people He has chosen, and in whom the Holy Spirit has revealed the truth about Jesus.

Second, Jesus says the church is built on a "rock" and there are various ways to interpret the meaning of the "rock." We can interpret the "rock" as

4. 1 Cor. 11:23.
5. 1 Cor. 7:10.
6. 1 Cor. 9:14.
7. Matt. 16:15.
8. Matt. 16:16.
9. Matt. 16:17-19.

Peter's confession. It is the confession that triggers Jesus's mention of the rock, and the church is built on the truth of that confession that Jesus is the Messiah, the Son of God. All who make this same confession—a profession of their faith in Christ—are members who build-up the church.

Or, in the simplest, and plainest reading of the text, Jesus could have meant that the church would be built on the "rock" personified by the apostle Peter. The name Peter, after all, is the Greek translation of the Aramaic: *Cephas*, meaning "stone" or "rock," the nickname that Jesus gave to Simon. Although Peter had moments when his faith teetered, it never failed him completely and, in the end, he was a rock-like man of faith that Jesus was willing to entrust with the task of doing the initial groundwork in building the church.

John Calvin interpreted this passage as Christ telling Peter that he would be the first of many rocks—believers—used to build the church. "Hence it is evident how this name Peter comes to be applied both to Simon individually, and to other believers ... For Christ, by announcing that this would be the common foundation of the whole Church, intended to associate with Peter all the godly that would ever exist in the world."[10] In other words, Jesus was saying to Peter, "I call you 'Rock' because you are like a rock—chipped, but not broken—and with trustworthy rocks like you I will build my church." Christ, as Isaiah prophesied, is the foundational cornerstone of the church,[11] but Peter was a "rock" in the foundation who had the honor of being the initial building block of the visible church.

In the Reformed tradition, however, this doesn't mean that Peter was made a super-apostle with supreme authority over all others. In fact, at times the Bible shows us Peter submitting to the authority of others or even being corrected on church matters. For example, in the Book of Acts we see the apostle James, not Peter, having the last word at the Jerusalem Council.[12] And, in Paul's letter to the Galatians, we see that Peter was admonished for his hypocrisy.[13] And nowhere in the Bible do we find evidence of successors to Peter becoming head of the church. In fact, the only head of the church that the Bible mentions is Jesus Christ.[14] Reformed theology,

---

10. Jean Calvin, *Calvin's Commentaries*, 291.
11. Is. 28:16.
12. Acts 15.
13. Galatians 2:11ff.
14. Ephesians 1:22; Col. 1:18.

therefore, views Peter not as the first infallible pope, but as an important, uniquely honored "rock" in the foundation of the church.

Third, Jesus tells us that He is the architect of the church. It is His church and He is the one who builds it: "... I will build *my* church."[15] Whenever we are tempted to disparage the church we should remember these words of Jesus. Before we become overly critical of the church we should remember it is Christ's idea, He is the one building it up, He loves the church as His bride, and He gave His life for it. "Husbands, love your wives, just as Christ loved the church and gave himself up for her."[16]

Fourth, Jesus says the church will be a force so powerful nothing can stop it from succeeding, not even the gates of Hades, i.e., the gates of death. If death is the last enemy,[17] and even *it* cannot overcome the church, then Jesus is saying the church will endure until the end of time. But the use of the term, "gates of Hades," adds additional meaning to what Jesus is saying about the enduring power of the church. In Jesus's day, cities were surrounded by walls and people entered the city through gates. These gates became the place where business meetings, public hearings, and court proceedings were held. The gates of Hades, therefore, symbolizes the place of business in the underworld where evil spirits and Satan conspire. Jesus is saying that evil powers will launch attacks on the church from the gates of Hades, but the enemies of the church will not prevail.

Finally, Jesus tells Peter that he will be given the keys to the kingdom of heaven and the power to "bind" and "loose." Here, Jesus is not saying that Peter decides who is allowed to enter heaven and who is not allowed. Rather, a key was symbolic of a scribe unlocking the meaning of Scripture. Jesus is indicating that Peter, by virtue of his teaching office, and as a minister of the Word of God in the church, has the keys—the teachings—that unlock the meaning of the gospel, thereby opening the door to belief and the kingdom of heaven.

Jesus railed against the Jewish teachers of religious law whose false doctrines took away the key of knowledge and prevented people from entering the kingdom.[18] In contrast to those false teachers, Jesus is letting Peter know that he, and all who are ministers of the Word of God, will be given opportunities to open the doors of the kingdom to both Jews and

---

15. Matt. 16:18, emphasis added.
16. Ephesians 5:25.
17. 1 Cor. 15:26.
18. Luke 11:52.

Gentiles by teaching the "Holy Scriptures, which are able to make you wise for salvation through faith in Christ Jesus."[19]

And that is what happened. Peter's sermon in Jerusalem on the Day of Pentecost was an outreach to the Jews that immediately added 3,000 believers to the church.[20] His sermon in Caesarea to Cornelius and his friends took the gospel to Gentiles.[21]

In Jewish and rabbinic terminology, "binding and loosing" referred to forbidding and permitting, respectively. It is notable in this passage that Jesus says, "whatever" you bind, not "whoever" you bind, indicating that He was talking about a declarative power to forbid or permit things or actions. Jesus was giving Peter, and later all the apostles,[22] the authority to declare the rites, ceremonies, rules, and other aspects of life in the church that are permitted or not permitted.

With the teaching they received from Jesus, and guided by the Holy Spirit dwelling within them, the apostles would be able to organize and govern the church knowing their decisions had the force of divine authority in heaven. We see this principle put into practice at the Jerusalem Council when the church is trying to decide if Gentile converts to the faith must be circumcised. The elders at the council permitted (loosed) the new believers to join the church without being circumcised, and they forbid (bound) them from eating "food sacrificed to idols."[23]

Together, the keys to the kingdom of heaven and the power to bind and loose constitute authority. With these few words Jesus indicates that the church will have a government; it will include people in positions of authority who lead it.

Later in Matthew's Gospel, Jesus again mentions the church when teaching His disciples how to handle disagreements between believers. He tells them to follow a three-step process to settle disputes. First, try to work it out with each other, just the two parties who disagree. If that doesn't work, get a committee of two or three to hear the argument. Then, as a last step turn to the authority of the church. "If they still refuse to listen, tell it to the church; and if they refuse to listen even to the church, treat them as you

---

19. 1 Tim. 3:15.
20. Acts 2.
21. Acts 10.
22. Matt. 18:18.
23. Acts 15:28.

would a pagan or a tax collector."[24] According to Jesus, those in positions of authority in the church must exercise discipline for the benefit of the whole church.

When these two passages are added to Jesus's commands to celebrate the Lord's Supper in remembrance of Him,[25] and to "go and make disciples of all nations, baptizing them in the name of the Father and of the Son and of the Holy Spirit, and teaching them to obey everything I have commanded you,"[26] we have enough to discern a primitive ecclesiology—the doctrine of the church—based on the teachings of Jesus. And it seems like this was the blueprint that Paul and the apostles used when planting the first Christian churches.

The earliest Christian churches, shaped by the teachings of Jesus passed on by the apostles, met in homes instead of synagogues,[27] marked new members with baptism instead of circumcision, gathered on the first day of the week instead of Saturday, and broke bread in the Lord's Supper to remember the death and resurrection of Jesus.[28] Reading Scripture,[29] preaching the gospel,[30] and proclaiming Jesus as the Messiah, the Son of God, were priorities for these churches. The churches appointed elders to preach, teach, and govern,[31] and deacons to care for their members.[32] Their time together included psalms, hymns, and spiritual songs,[33] prayer,[34] teaching and fellowship,[35] discipline,[36] and taking up an offering to fund the church.[37]

---

24. Matt. 18:17.
25. Luke 22:19.
26. Matt. 28:19-20.
27. Romans 16:5.
28. Acts 20:7.
29. 1 Tim. 4:13.
30. 1 Cor. 15:1.
31. Acts 14:23.
32. 1 Tim. 3:8-10; Philippians 1:1.
33. Col. 3:16.
34. 1 Thess. 5:17.
35. Acts 2:42.
36. Galatians 6:1.
37. 1 Cor. 16:1-2.

Part V: Structure

Reformed Ecclesiology

By 1517, when the German priest named Martin Luther started his push for the church to address issues he felt needed reform, what had started as a simple weekly gathering in someone's home to pray, sing, read Scripture, and break bread in remembrance of Jesus, had evolved into the Mass. The service was now presided over by a priest who was wearing special vestments, standing at an altar, and speaking in Latin, "a language that almost no one in the pews and many in the pulpit could understand."[38] In the Mass, ". . . only the priest now took the wine. Members of the congregation came and knelt before him to receive the wafer. So solemn was the service that the people usually took communion once a year only."[39] They could, however, request a special Mass "for their own souls, for the souls of dead relatives or as a means of requesting God's assistance for particular problems. Masses were said for peace in time of war, for fair weather during harvest, recovery from illness and even for the curing of sick farm animals. Very often a fee was charged for such services."[40] The Reformers, finding no biblical basis for what the Mass had become, felt there was a need for significant changes to the way the sixteenth century church was operating.

When the community celebrates the Lord's Supper, for example, the Reformers thought wine as well as the bread should be given to those participating. Scripture, prayers, and songs should be in the native language of those who are worshiping. Churches should be led by pastors who are skilled at preaching and teaching the Word of God to the people, instead of priests who mediate between the people and God. And the Reformers believed pastors should be able to marry, if they so desire, since celibacy is not a biblical requirement.

These were real and noticeable modifications to the status quo, but Martin Luther's initial concern was not the development of a whole new church. He remained confident the adjustments being called for would re-form the already existing Catholic church and bring it back toward the model found in the New Testament. The hope was that the church would return to a simpler service, more accessible to the faithful and more focused on preaching what the apostle Paul said is "of first importance: that Christ died for our sins according to the Scriptures, that he was buried, that he

---

38. Stark, *The Triumph of Christianity*, 265.
39. Marshall, *John Knox*, Kindle location 615.
40. Ibid.

was raised on the third day according to the Scriptures."[41] In the decades following Luther's reformation efforts, however, it became apparent that re-forming the existing church was not possible; a whole new Reformed ecclesiology began to take shape.

The Reformation was staked on justification through faith alone, in Christ alone, which negated much of what had been added to the church. In the mind of the Reformers, salvation did not require the Mass, prayers to saints, sacraments, or the mediation of a priest in the church. As the apostle Paul said, "Everyone who calls on the name of the Lord will be saved."[42] So, the church needed to get back to its most important task: to make the name of Jesus Christ known throughout the world, otherwise, Paul asks, "How, then, can they call on the one they have not believed in? And how can they believe in the one of whom they have not heard? And how can they hear without someone preaching to them?"[43] The Holy Spirit uses the Word of God written, or preached, to change hearts, and the Reformers believed that's what the church should be focused on. In the Reformed tradition, the church is a community of faith where the gospel of Jesus Christ is preached, the sacraments are rightly administered, and believers are taught and charitably disciplined to live as becomes a follower of Christ.

The community of faith—the visible church—is made up of all who profess faith in Christ, and who come together to worship God and serve Him. In his sermon on the Day of Pentecost, the apostle Peter made it known that the children of those who profess their faith are also part of the visible church. "The promise is for you and your children..."[44]

It is in the visible church that we get a glimpse of the kingdom of God. Jesus started his ministry by proclaiming, "The kingdom of God has come near. Repent and believe the good news!"[45] The kingdom of God is the long-awaited Messianic rule, the age to come breaking into the present age right now. With Jesus, the kingdom has arrived; it hasn't been fully installed, but Jesus is King right now, sitting in the seat of highest cosmic authority, so His church should evidence His kingdom. The church should be a reflection of the life of King Jesus who healed the sick, fed the hungry, defeated demons, and offered sinners a chance to repent and come to God

---

41. 1 Cor. 15:3-4.
42. Romans 10:13.
43. Romans 10:14.
44. Acts 2:39.
45. Mark 1:15.

in faith. Therefore, each local congregation should be an outpost on the ever-expanding frontier of the kingdom where it cares for the sick, feeds the hungry, and ministers to lost souls. Church members should be encouraged and equipped to bear witness to Christ's kingship in every aspect of life including their jobs, families, schools, recreation, and finances.

Critics of the church are quick to point out the obvious: the church does not always live up to its great calling. It is not always the best example of the kingdom of God breaking into this world. This is not a surprise, however, since each saint who comprises the church is also a sinner; the visible church is an imperfect church. Particular parts of the visible church are more or less pure, as Jesus made clear in the letters to the seven churches found in the second and third chapters of the Book of Revelation.

But it is also true that over the centuries the church has made the kingdom of God quite visible. In ancient Roman society pagan philosophers regarded mercy as a "character defect and pity as a pathological emotion,"[46] but Christians were noticeably not like the rest of society. They not only showed love and mercy to their own families, they were charitable to those outside of the church too. "The Christians . . . ran a miniature welfare state in an empire which for the most part lacked social services."[47] From the earliest days, Christians have seen it as their duty to obey the teaching of Jesus who said, "For I was hungry and you gave me something to eat, I was thirsty and you gave me something to drink, I was a stranger and you invited me in, I needed clothes and you clothed me, I was sick and you looked after me, I was in prison and you came to visit me . . . Truly I tell you, whatever you did for one of the least of these brothers and sisters of mine, you did for me."[48]

The Reformers agreed with the church fathers that outside of the visible church there is no ordinary possibility of salvation: *extra ecclesiam nulla salus*—no salvation outside the church. Of course, they understood that church membership itself does not save us, but God has established the church as an instrument to bring salvation to the world. Clunky as it may be at times, the church is the way God has chosen to gather and perfect the saints, empowering them by the Holy Spirit to share the gospel as a witness for Jesus "in Jerusalem, and in all Judea and Samaria, and to the ends of the earth."[49]

---

46. Stark, 112.
47. Johnson, *A History of Christianity* in Stark, *The Triumph of Christianity*, 113.
48. Matt. 25:35-36, 40.
49. Acts 1:8.

Normally, those saved will publicly profess faith and be active in the church. In the New Testament there is no evidence of a churchless Christian, converts were baptized into Christ and into a visible body of believers. Cyprian, the third century martyr bishop of Carthage in North Africa said, "He who would have God as his Father must have the Church as his mother," and in Reformed theology the church is held in the same high regard.

With the Spirit of Christ dwelling within every believer, they are united to Christ and to each other to form the body of Christ on earth. And, just as Christ came into the world so that whoever believes in Him will be saved,[50] so the body of Christ is the continuing presence of the Incarnation that attracts, gathers, and saves believers.

As members of the body of Christ believers have both benefits and obligations to one another. The Spirit bestows gifts on each believer and these gifts are to be used for the benefit of the whole body, "Now to each one the manifestation of the Spirit is given for the common good."[51] Paul reminded the church in Thessalonica to "encourage one another and build each other up."[52] So, the church is not a consumer-driven enterprise—it's not just about me and what I need. Christians should not attend a church based solely on what they individually get out of it, they should attend a church to offer themselves "as a living sacrifice, holy and pleasing to God—this is your true and proper worship."[53] And we should keep in mind that a decision to not attend and participate in a local church is a decision to not share our God-given gifts with other members of the church, and not contribute to the communal worship that brings glory to God, and comfort and strength to our brothers and sisters in Christ.

Church Government

When we attend a local church, we encounter an organization whose structure of authority comes from Christ. The apostle Paul tells us that "Christ himself gave the apostles, the prophets, the evangelists, the pastors and teachers, to equip his people for works of service, so that the body of Christ may be built up . . ."[54] These were the names of the offices that presided over

50. John 3:16.
51. 1 Cor. 12:7.
52. 1 Thess. 5:11.
53. Romans 12:1.
54. Ephesians 4:11-12.

and governed the church as it began to take the gospel into the world. But in Reformed theology the first three of these offices were temporary.

John Calvin understood the apostles, prophets, and evangelists, as offices established by Christ for a unique purpose "at the beginning," and while He "still occasionally raises them up when the necessity of the times require," they "were not instituted in the church to be perpetual, but only to endure so long as the churches were to be formed where none previously existed..."[55] In Calvin's Reformed ecclesiology, the church is now presided over and governed by the last two on Paul's list: pastors and teachers, both of whom hold the perpetual office of elder.

In the Acts of the Apostles we read that Paul and Barnabas went to Lystra, Iconium, and Antioch, where they "appointed elders for them in each church."[56] And Paul told Titus to "appoint elders in every town."[57] At times, Paul would call the elders overseers (from the Greek word for bishop), or shepherds (from the Greek word for pastor), such as when he addresses the elders of the church in Ephesus for the last time, "Keep watch over yourselves and all the flock of which the Holy Spirit has made you *overseers*. Be *shepherds* of the church of God, which he bought with his own blood."[58] So, whether they were called overseers, bishops, shepherds, or pastors, the leaders of the first century churches held the office of elder.

The Greek word for "elder" is *presbuteros* from which we get the word "Presbyterian." In its simplest, earliest form, the New Testament church, ruled by elders or "presbyters," was "Presbyterian" in structure. Like the first century churches that the apostle Paul started, John Calvin believed the form of government in sixteenth century Reformed churches should be Presbyterian, and those who met to write the Westminster Confession of Faith in the middle of the seventeenth century also favored the Presbyterian form of government.

While all elders are called to oversee the spiritual and doctrinal health of the church, to pray with and for the church, and to teach the Scriptures to church members, according to the apostle Paul there are two distinct roles within the one office of elder. He makes the distinction in his first letter to Timothy. "The *elders who direct the affairs of the church* well are worthy

---

55. Calvin, *Institutes*, 702-703.
56. Acts 14:23.
57. Titus 1:5.
58. Acts 20:28, emphasis added.

of double honor, especially *those whose work is preaching and teaching*."[59] Here we see that all elders direct the affairs—govern—the church. Some of those elders, however, are especially gifted at preaching and teaching. Those elders who are primarily concerned with directing the affairs of the church are called ruling elders in today's Reformed churches. Those elders who, in addition to governing the church, also work at preaching and teaching, are called teaching elders. The pastor of a church is selected from the teaching elders because the primary task of a pastor is preaching the gospel, whether in a sermon or through the administration of the sacraments. The emphases of the ruling and teaching elder ministries are slightly different, but their jurisdiction and authority are the same; they hold the same office.

In addition to the ministry of the elders, Christ has given the church the ministry of the deacons. The office of deacon is a perpetual office in the church distinct from the elders in that deacons serve in a ministry of mercy and deed, whereas elders serve in a ministry of the Word. For example, when there was a dispute about the way food was being distributed to widows in the first century church, deacons were selected to resolve the problem so that the elders could give their "attention to prayer and the ministry of the word."[60] Because the church is called to love and support one another in both spiritual and material ways, Reformed churches establish diaconal mercy ministries.

References to church leaders in the New Testament are plural, which is a good indication that the pastor of a church should not lead alone. In the Reformed tradition the pastor joins with the ruling elders to form what is called the session (or board of elders), and together they govern and shepherd the church. With the pastor as the moderator, the session meets regularly to oversee the spiritual health of the church. The session receives members into the communion of the church, examines, ordains, and installs church officers, makes decisions regarding the budget and church property, and exercises authority over the ordinances of the church—the God-ordained functions specifically for the church such as worship, teaching, reading Scripture, the sacraments, and discipline.

Also, in the New Testament we see that the various churches seemed to be related to one another; none of them were isolated churches. For example, Paul appealed to the church in Corinth and the churches in the province of

---

59. 1 Tim. 5:17, emphasis added.
60. Acts 6:4.

Galatia to take up a gift offering in support of the church in Jerusalem.[61] And representatives from the various churches assembled in councils to decide theological debates, such as when Paul and Barnabas went with a group of selected church members to Jerusalem to consult with the apostles and elders there regarding the necessity of circumcision for salvation.[62]

The example of the earliest church found in the New Testament does not seem to allow for a congregational form of church government where individual pastors or church boards operate autonomously with little or no association with other churches. Interestingly, however, by the end of the first century the Presbyterian form of the early church had morphed into an Episcopal organization, from the Greek: *episkopos*, meaning bishop. The pastors of influential churches in Smyrna, Ephesus, and Rome had become the bishops that other church leaders continued to look to for guidance and, eventually, the bishop of Rome became the most powerful in the West. Even so, the Reformed tradition continues to favor the Presbyterian form of government at both the local and regional level, like what we find in the primitive church.

In the New Testament, members of the church were involved in choosing their leaders. In the Book of Acts, we see church members choosing the first deacons.[63] And later, the church participated in selecting the men who would deliver and communicate the findings of the Jerusalem Council regarding circumcision.[64] Reformed churches follow this example by asking members to prayerfully seek guidance from the Holy Spirit in nominating those whose character, family life, doctrinal maturity, and ability to teach, meet the biblical qualifications of elder or deacon. Once nominated by the members of the church, the elders currently serving on the session further examine the candidates and then present those deemed ready to serve to the congregation for a final vote. In this way, leadership in a Reformed church is established through a process of mutual discernment among members and elders, with reliance upon the guidance of the Holy Spirit.

The Presbyterian form of church government provides layers of accountability. Members of the church choose the elders who will be their overseers. Churches within a geographical area form and report to a Presbytery. Then, once each year ruling and teaching elders from all the

---

61. 1 Cor. 16:1-3.
62. Acts 15.
63. Acts 6:3.
64. Acts 15:22.

Presbyteries meet at a General Assembly to conduct the business of the entire church.

Since members play such a vital role in determining the leadership of a Reformed church, official membership in a local congregation is taken seriously. Everyone is welcome to join the congregation in its worship, prayer, and fellowship activities, but full membership, with all of its rights and privileges, is reserved for those who have made a profession of faith in Christ, have been baptized, and have been admitted by the elders to participate in the Lord's Supper.

All members agree to strive for the purity and peace of the church with the full understanding that one of the marks of a Reformed church is the exercise of discipline. Discipline is not punishment; it is meant to restore to full, active church participation, repentant spiritual brothers and sisters who seriously stray from their promise to strive to live as becomes a follower of Christ. To exercise discipline is to recognize that every member of the church falls short of the holiness that God has called them to, and holding each other accountable in an orderly and discrete way is the best way to deter spiritual brothers and sisters from serious sin. Done properly, church discipline combines truth and love, and respects the teaching of the apostle Peter who said, "Above all, love each other deeply, because love covers over a multitude of sins."[65] By lovingly applying biblical discipline the church vindicates the honor of Christ, because the church is the body of Christ in the world, and serious sin left unchecked brings Him dishonor.

Worship

Reformed churches are simple in décor and worship style. There are few candles, and you will not typically find incense, clerical robes, liturgical colors, or art work on the walls. Presbyterians are characteristically a stoic bunch and, depending on your perspective, the blame, or the credit, can especially be put on two sixteenth century men named John.

For John Calvin (1509-1564), the Reformation was just as much about recapturing a knowledge of how God is properly worshiped as it was about how we are saved. In fact, he believed "there is nothing more perilous to our salvation than a preposterous and perverse worship of God."[66] And it

---

65. 1 Peter 4:8.
66. Calvin, *Tracts Relating to the Reformation*, trans. Henry Beveridge, 1:126 in Robert Kolb and Carl R. Trueman, *Between Wittenberg and Geneva*, 223.

was in Scripture that the nature of true and proper worship could be found, "for Calvin it was God's Word that was to regulate the form and content of our worship."[67] Therefore, Calvin instituted the "regulative principle" of worship in the church he pastored at Geneva, Switzerland. This regulative principle of worship permitted only those things that Scripture requires because, "It is abomination in the sight of God to frame to him a worship which he does not require, or to embrace one devised by man without the sanction of his word."[68]

John Knox (1513-1572) passionately applied John Calvin's regulative principle to worship in the Reformed churches of England and Scotland. Knox studied 1 Samuel 15 and noted the consequences that King Saul suffered when he offered in worship to God the plunder from his victory over the Amalekites instead of obeying God and destroying it all on the battlefield. For his disobedience and, as Calvin might say, his "perverse" worship of God, Saul was punished with the loss of his kingdom to David. John Knox saw in that story the importance of strictly adhering to the regulative principle: do not worship God with anything other than what God requires, no matter how well-intentioned it may seem. For the Reformers, strict adherence to the regulative principle of worship was a matter of being obedient to the Word of God.

The regulative principle of worship also started to establish a clear distinction between church and state. Prior to the Reformation, the church and the state were one and the same. But, by insisting that the form and content of worship was based solely on what Scripture required, the church "delimited the power of the state with regard to the church's worship and indeed also the power of the church to demand conformity to extraneous rites not built on a scriptural foundation."[69]

With the regulative principle in mind, the Westminster Confession of Faith mentions five elements required for proper worship: prayer, reading and hearing Scripture, preaching Scripture, singing psalms, and administering the sacraments.[70] In the Reformed tradition, if these five elements do not constitute the core of your church's regular worship practices you should consider whether your worship is God-honoring. And, although "religious oaths, vows, solemn fasting, and thanksgiving" are acceptable

---

67. Kolb and Trueman, 224.
68. Calvin, *Antidote to the Articles* in Kolb and Trueman, 226.
69. Kolb and Trueman, 227.
70. WCF 21.3-5.

means of worship "on special occasions,"[71] in the strictest sense of the regulative principle, if you add something to the essential elements of worship, you risk experiencing the disfavor of God, just like King Saul.

Certainly, then, anything that is explicitly prohibited in Scripture cannot be included in worship. Therefore, because God prohibited the creation of carved images or likenesses of anything in heaven,[72] the Reformers eliminated stained glass, statues, images of Christ, and crucifixes in the church. No wonder worship in Reformed churches can seem so simple and dispassionate; they are greatly concerned to worship in the way God has instructed us to worship Him.

I like the idea of using Scripture to regulate our worship, but I personally do not believe the regulative principle is meant to restrict the creativity and diversity of worship. After all, the apostle Paul told the church in Colossae to sing hymns and spiritual songs, as well as, psalms.[73] And it appears that Paul allowed for the collection of an offering as a part of worship.[74] But hymns, spiritual songs, and offerings are not explicitly mentioned in the chapter on worship in the Westminster Confession of Faith.

Scripture should be our guide to good worship practices, but we would not expect worship, breathed out by the Holy Spirit through people of various cultures, at various times, to always and everywhere look and sound the same. The Reformers emphasized the inward, spiritual aspect of worship. As Jesus put it, "true worshipers will worship the Father in the Spirit and in truth."[75] To worship in the Spirit is to come before God, who is spirit, and offer all of ourselves to Him "as a living sacrifice."[76] To worship in truth is to worship without dependence on the temple and the temporary ceremonies and sacrifices of the Old Testament law. They all pointed forward to the worship of Jesus Christ, who is the Truth.

That means worship is not just about going through a checklist of right activities; there is a sense in which the correct elements and form of worship must go together with a genuine inward devotion to God. Worship must be done from the heart, conscientiously obedient to God, with faith and holiness. And this can be done in a way that involves all of our senses,

---

71. WCF 21.5.
72. Exodus 20:4; Deuteronomy 5:8.
73. Col. 3:16.
74. 2 Cor. 9:7; 8:19.
75. John 4:23.
76. Romans 12:1.

or it can be done in an aesthetically simple—regulated—way, both of which can be beautiful.

The Presbyterian church where I am an elder and where I worship every Sunday has a much different look and feel than the Catholic church where I was an altar boy in my youth. I am comfortable in both settings; sometimes I long for the smell of incense and the changing colors of the church calendar, but I also appreciating the simplicity of my current church. We do not have statues and stained-glass windows, but our Creative Director and his team produce some of the most beautiful worship settings I have seen. Using their God-given gifts of artistry and design they combine texture, light, color, and sound to help focus the congregation's attention on God and the preaching of His Word. Our music can be contemporary, ancient, electric, or acoustic. The sacraments are administered simply, but powerfully. My brothers and sisters in Christ are certainly more stoic than charismatic when they gather together to worship, but I do not believe that Christ would walk into our church and be anything but delighted by what He saw and heard.

Conclusion

Thomas M. Tasselmyer

On the night before He died Jesus prayed for unity among His followers and in the church they would establish after His resurrection and ascension, "My prayer is not for them alone. I pray also for those who will believe in me through their message . . . that they may be brought to complete unity."[1] Contemplating His life, His friends, the mission He came to accomplish, and His imminent death, Jesus was expressing to His Father in heaven the deepest feelings of His heart. He was just hours away from suffering the brutality of the cross and yet, unity was at the top of His mind. But how should we hear this prayer for unity from Jesus? Did He expect uniformity in His church?

In chapter five I tried to construct a minimal Jesus ecclesiology from the few statements He made about the church, but I don't think that means we can look to the Bible to find a comprehensive "Jesus Instruction Manual" for running each and every church. Actually, I find it hard to imagine that Jesus expected absolute uniformity in the church because He said very little about how it should organize its worship, leadership, finances, and all other aspects of its day-to-day operation. It seems to me that if He wanted uniformity He would have given us a New Testament version of the Book of Leviticus to ensure that every church would look and function in precisely the same manner, but He did not.

I think the unity that Jesus prayed for comes from the spiritual oneness that He spoke of when He said, "I pray . . . that all of them may be one, Father, just as you are in me and I am in you . . . I have given them the glory that you gave me, that they may be one as we are one . . ."[2] Jesus prayed for the oneness of the church to reflect the oneness between Him and His

1. John 17: 20,23.
2. John 17: 20-22.

Father, and this unity comes because His Holy Spirit dwells in me, and in you, and in every other Christian.

When we become a Christian through faith in Christ a new life begins. "I have been crucified with Christ and I no longer live, but Christ lives in me."[3] And with the Spirit of Christ inside of us, we are called to live our new life as part of the one mystical body of Christ—inseparably united to Him and to our Christian brothers and sisters. Thus, the church can be unified by the Spirit from the inside even though it is not necessarily uniform according to outward appearances and practices.

After all, the Holy Spirit who brings unity to the church by dwelling within each member, is the same Spirit who was there at the creation of the world as the Lord and Giver of life in all of its various and beautiful forms. He is the same Spirit who breathed life into hundreds of thousands of different flowers, birds, fish, animals, and billions upon billions of unique people. That same Spirit unifies the manifold expressions of the church. If the Holy Spirit, who is more creative than any human can imagine, is at work every day building, animating, and uniting the church, we should expect the same variety we see throughout creation to be evident in the church. We should not be surprised, or disappointed; instead, we should embrace and appreciate the great variety we find in the way the church looks, sounds, and functions throughout the world. And we should flee any inclination for the church's outward variety to produce disdain, rivalry, or hatred in us, for in so doing we bring injury to the body of Christ and dishonor to the Spirit.

Unfortunately, the church is made up of fallen people and maintaining unity has proved to be a struggle from the very beginning. The earliest church wrestled with how Jewish the new faith should remain; they were divided over whether they could eat the same food that Gentiles eat and whether they could even associate with Gentiles, and if Gentiles were allowed to convert, whether they must be circumcised when they joined the church. The apostle Paul had to admonish the church in Corinth for the divisiveness created when they quarreled over preferences to follow one leader or another, "One of you says, 'I follow Paul'; another, 'I follow Apollos'; another, 'I follow Cephas'; still another, 'I follow Christ.' Is Christ divided? Was Paul crucified for you? Were you baptized in the name of Paul?"[4] Paul knew the importance of the church remaining unified but

3. Galatians 2:20.
4. 1 Cor. 1:12-13.

Conclusion

his insistence on unity centered around loyalty to Christ alone. And, in the ensuing centuries, as the church grew and spread into the world, other issues arose and produced disagreements and disunity including: Docetism, Gnosticism, and Arianism to name a few.[5]

The church's classical response to these divisive issues was to set them against the faith of the apostles to see if they contradicted or upheld what the church had always believed and taught. But after the last of the apostles died and they could no longer be consulted, the church had to turn to other church leaders to continue the process.

The leaders of the church after the apostles died were known as Fathers of the church. They can be separated into the "Apostolic Fathers," and a later group who could be called the "Church Fathers."[6] The Apostolic Fathers cover a period of about one hundred years dating back to the first and second centuries. Traditionally it is believed that these Christians were personally close to one or more of the original apostles, or an acquaintance of an apostle. We find the writings of the Apostolic Fathers in the *Letter of Barnabas*, the *Didache*, the *Letters* of Ignatius of Antioch, the *Letter of Polycarp*, the *Martyrdom of Polycarp*, the first and second letters of Clement of Rome, the *Shepherd of Hermas*, and the *Letter to Diognetus*.

The Church Fathers were the group of influential Christians that followed in the footsteps of the Apostolic Fathers and it "has become customary to delineate four main criteria to identify [them]: they must be ancient, orthodox in doctrine, holy in life, and approved by other Christians."[7] Or, using the wisdom of the fifth century French monk Vincent of Lerins, to be accepted as a Church Father, an author must pass along "what has been believed everywhere, always, and by all."[8] In other words the Church Fathers

---

5. Docetism is the belief that Jesus was a spirit who only appeared to have a body. Gnosticism is an extreme dualism creating a distinction between the body and the spirit with humans trapped in their "evil" physical body, only able to be released from it through a special *gnosis*, or divine knowledge. Arianism holds that Jesus was not fully God, he was not of one essence, nature, or substance with God, and therefore not like Him, or equal in dignity, or co-eternal, or within the real sphere of Deity.

6. Bryan Liftin notes there were Church Mothers who made major contributions to Christianity too, "great women in the ancient church . . . especially martyrs and virgins who lived consecrated lives before God," such as Perpetua, who was martyred in 203 CE, but since "in ancient society, women were rarely taught to read and write . . . few women's writings have come down to us today from the early church period," *Getting to Know the Church Fathers: An Evangelical Introduction*, p.17.

7. Litfin, *Getting to Know the Church Fathers*, 19.

8. Ibid.

are "those who lived righteously and passed down to later generations the core tenets of the Christian faith that they themselves had received from the apostles."[9] Five Church Fathers that greatly influenced Christianity in the first three centuries were: Justin Martyr, Irenaeus of Lyons, Hippolytus of Rome, Tertullian, and Origen.

So, Jesus taught His apostles and sent them into the world to build the church and teach others what they had learned from Him. The apostles passed the teaching of Jesus on to the Fathers of the church and they took the initiative to preserve the teaching in creeds; short, easily memorized summaries of the apostolic faith. The creeds came to be known as "The Rule of Faith," the benchmark of what all Christians, everywhere, have always believed. The Rule of Faith was used in teaching new members the beliefs they were required to profess when being baptized to join the church and in addressing schisms that threatened to divide the church. I believe this is the direction we need to go as we seek to understand what divides us while embracing what unites us. So, what is the Rule of Faith that should unite us?

By about the year 190 Irenaeus of Lyons was teaching the Rule of Faith in a creed that we could still embrace as a unifying statement of faith today:

> The Church, though dispersed throughout the world, even to the ends of the earth, has received from the apostles, and their disciples, this faith:
>
> [She believes] in one God, the Father Almighty, Maker of heaven, and earth, and the sea, and all things that are in them;
>
> And in one Christ Jesus, the Son of God, who became incarnate for our salvation;
>
> And in the Holy Spirit, who proclaimed through the prophets the dispensations of God.
>
> (*Against Heresies*, 1.10.1)

When Irenaeus's creed was refined by the highly influential church in Rome it became known as *The Old Roman Rule* or *Roman Symbol*, and by the end of the second century what we know today as the Apostles' Creed had essentially taken shape:

> I believe in God the Father almighty, Creator of heaven and earth;
> And in Jesus Christ, His only Son, our Lord,
> who was conceived by the Holy Spirit, born from the Virgin Mary,
> suffered under Pontius Pilate, was crucified, dead and buried.
> He descended to hell. On the third day He rose again from the dead,

---

9. Ibid.

Conclusion

He ascended to heaven, sits at the right hand of God the Father almighty,
and from there He will come to judge the living and the dead.
I believe in the Holy Spirit,
the holy catholic church,
the communion of saints,
the forgiveness of sins,
the resurrection of the body,
and life everlasting. Amen.[10]

The Apostles' Creed, then, was not written by the Apostle's themselves but it contains a summary of the church's teaching dating back to "apostolic" times and it remains, perhaps, the most ecumenical creed we have. Accepted by Protestants, Roman Catholics, and Orthodox alike it summarizes what we all believe using just 110 words. Here is the Rule of Faith that the Church Father, Origen of Alexandria (185-254), considered the basis and guide for our theology. He called the Apostles' Creed "the teaching of the church, transmitted in orderly succession from the apostles, and remaining in the churches to the present day, still preserved, that alone is to be accepted as truth which differs in no respect from the ecclesiastical and apostolical tradition" (*First Principles*, Preface, 2).

However, even as the Apostles' Creed gained influence as a statement of faith that unified the church, the Roman Emperor Constantine found it necessary to convene the Council of Nicea on June 19, 325 with the goal of consolidating various factions that were still developing in the church, especially the one associated with the Arian controversy that originated in 318.

Arius was a priest in the city of Alexandria, Egypt, who was found to be teaching that the Son of God was subordinate to the Father. Arianism, as the controversy came to be called, was a heretical rejection of orthodox teaching regarding the Trinity. For Arius and his followers, the three Persons of the Trinity "were utterly different beings, and did not share in any way the same substance or essence as each other."[11] Emperor Constantine reminded the 300 or so bishops in attendance at the council that "division in the church . . . was worse than war," and they needed little time to debate; the controversy of Arianism was quickly settled.[12] The statement of faith

---

10. The phrase, "He descended to hell" first appears in about 404 CE in a commentary on the Creed by Rufinus of Aquileia, an apparent reference to 1 Peter 3:18-20.
11. Kelly, *Early Christian Creeds*, 234.
12. Shelley, *Church History in Plain Language*, 101.

they produced was the Creed of Nicea, the first draft of what we now know as the Nicene Creed. It was signed by all but two of the bishops present and they, along with Arius, were sent into exile, but the Arian controversy would not go away.

Supporters of Arianism, or a more moderate Semi-Arianism, argued against Athanasius, the bishop of Alexandria, and his supporters, who believed Christ was not only "like" the Father, He was actually of the "same" nature as the Father. To reaffirm the faith of Nicea and its repudiation of Arianism, and to counter new heresies, another church council was held in 381, this time in Constantinople. The Council of Constantinople used the ideas and framework of the creed formulated in Nicea and produced the final draft of the Nicene Creed or, perhaps more accurately called, the Nicene-Constantinopolitan Creed. In it we find that Athanasius argued successfully to use the Greek word "*homoousios*" meaning "same" or "one substance" to describe the relationship between Christ and the Father, instead of the word Arius would have preferred, "*homoiousios*" meaning "like substance." The importance of this one word, indeed of the one letter "i" that differentiates the two contested words, cannot be understated as "there were Christians willing to face exile and even death to keep this one letter out of the Creed."[13] By stating that Jesus Christ is of one substance with the Father, the Nicene-Constantinopolitan Creed definitively protected the unique oneness of God:

> We believe in one God, the Father almighty, maker of heaven and earth, of all things visible and invisible;And in one Lord Jesus Christ, the only-begotten Son of God, begotten from the Father before all time, Light from Light, True God from True God, begotten not made, of the same substance as the Father, through Whom all things were made, who for us men and for our salvation came down from heaven and was incarnate by the Holy Spirit and the Virgin Mary, and became human. He was crucified for us under Pontius Pilate, and suffered, and was buried, and rose on the third day, according to the scriptures, and ascended to heaven, and sits on the right hand of the Father, and will come again with glory to judge the living and dead. His kingdom shall have no end. And in the Holy Spirit, the Lord and Giver of life, who proceeds from the Father, who together with the Father and the Son is worshipped and glorified, who spoke through the prophets. And in one, holy,

---

13. Coniaris, *Orthodoxy*, 88.

Conclusion

catholic, and apostolic church. We confess one baptism for the forgiveness of sins.

We look forward to the resurrection of the dead and the life of the world to come. Amen.

Like the Apostles' Creed, the Nicene-Constantinopolitan Creed is a statement of faith that all Christians can actually recite and agree on; it is a powerful unifying force that holds us together even as we express our faith in many and various ways. It is a consensus of Christian belief that frees us to disagree on various issues without compromising orthodoxy.[14]

However, we still have to do some work; these creeds don't explain the details of what we believe. They send us to Scripture to do theology and discover what it really means to say that we believe Jesus is the Christ, the Son of God, and our Lord; that He was incarnate by the Holy Spirit and the Virgin Mary; that the Holy Spirit may be worshipped and glorified; that there will be a resurrection of the dead, etc. And the creeds are not plenary surveys of all the issues a Christian may contemplate.

But our views on whatever is not found in them, the canon of Scripture, the sacraments, the atonement, the structure of the church, to cite a few examples, turn out to be non-essential opinions and preferences. Our differences on the non-essentials may be important and significant, but if what I am teaching does not contradict or oppose the direct or implied truths found in the Apostles or Nicene creeds, what I am teaching is probably allowable and you and I can be Christians who simply agree to disagree. We can reach different conclusions on some weighty issues and still support one another, unified in one, holy, catholic, and apostolic church; a gathering of God's people called out to fulfill His purposes. Using the creeds as a guardrail over which we plunge into heresy, we can have theological disagreements and remain a catholic church that is universal in its nature, open to all people from all cultures, races, and backgrounds, encompassing many styles, traditions,

---

14. The original Nicene-Constantinopolitan Creed of 381 declared the Holy Spirit "proceeds from the Father", alluding to John 15:26: "When the Counselor comes, whom I will send to you from the Father, the Spirit of truth who goes out from the Father, he will testify about me" (NIV). But in 589, at the Third Council of Toledo, the Latin phrase "*filioque*" meaning "and the Son" was inserted. With the *filioque* addition, the Creed states the Holy Spirit "proceeds from the Father and the Son". Latin writing theologians in the west held the double-procession, *filioque* position, most explicitly, while Greek writing theologians in the east tended to reject it. The east-west split over the *filioque* worsened through the ninth century and remains today.

and denominations, unified by one Spirit, and forming one body of Christ with a common confession of one gospel.

The danger comes when we become over-confident and proud of our theology. For the church to be united in the way that Jesus prayed for, we should take a lesson from the two despondent travelers on the road to Emmaus on the first Easter Sunday. Until the events of Good Friday they were sure their theology was pretty good. Then Jesus died and that didn't make sense to them—their theology fell apart. In fact, when the risen Jesus appears on the road with them unrecognized, He calls them "foolish" and "slow to believe" and He graciously conducts a remedial theology course on the spot, "beginning with Moses and all the Prophets, he explained to them what was said in all the Scriptures concerning himself."[15] I have to believe that when Jesus returns class will be in session, again, and all of us will see Jesus smile, and hear Him chuckle at how foolish some of our own theology is. For me, that will actually be quite enjoyable. Until Christ returns, however, it's probably wise to use whatever strife arises between Christians as a warning sign that pride is getting the best of us. "Where there is strife, there is pride, but wisdom is found in those who take advice."[16]

The unity of Persons in the Trinity is our example for unity in the church. All three persons of the Trinity are God; equal in power, glory, and dignity. Like our triune God, all Christians who confess our common creed are equal. We are not in competition. We are called to strive for a unity of purpose in the body of Christ even as perfect unity will only be truly manifested when Christ returns. So, let's study God's Word, explain our opinions, and seek to understand each other with an irenic spirit, conscious that arguments and animosity present a negative witness to the world.

This book was written to help us understand some of the issues that have historically divided large segments of the church and produced the animosity that harms the body and dishonors the Spirit. My hope is that a fuller understanding of these issues will help us see that we can have unity, and diversity, because we have a common creed that unifies us against a common foe, "For our struggle is not against flesh and blood, but against the rulers, against the authorities, against the powers of this dark world and against the spiritual forces of evil in the heavenly realms."[17]

---

15. Luke 24: 25, 27.
16. Proverbs 13:10.
17. Ephesians 6:12.

Lyle K. Weiss

ONE OF THE FIRST things my wife learned about my family is that we seem born to argue and debate. I come from one of those families that seems capable of debating just about any topic under the sun. When I introduced my then fiancé to my family, the debate topics du jour were the reality of ghosts, the reality of extraterrestrials, whether professional wrestling was real, and whether Tim Duncan, then playing for the Wake Forest basketball program, would make a good pro. A shouting match ensued when that last topic was raised, with one of my brothers insisting at the top of his voice that Duncan would never be a good pro. I like to think it was those dispiriting words from my brother that inspired Duncan to the heights of NBA glory and that therefore we had something to do with his remarkable success. (Mr. Duncan, if you are reading this, please feel free to contact me through the publisher.) Needless to say, debates were a way of life in my family. It took me years to decide I would no longer participate in those debates, given that they never seemed to accomplish anything, that they were never really about anything other than winning, and that I had come to the realization that I no longer needed to prove the rightness of my beliefs.

In my humble opinion, my family does not know how to debate. My late father was expert at simply making up statistics to support his cause. Once, while debating the origins of the Civil War, he suggested slavery had nothing to do with it and that 95% of American History professors agreed. When pressed for sources, he stated he had read it somewhere. No doubt the history professors throughout the country would have been surprised by that fictive statistic. But, fabricated statistics and facts, what the Trump administration would call 'alternative facts,' were perfectly acceptable because the point of my family's debates was not the pursuit of truth but the quest for victory. It did not matter whether debates made us all more thoughtful people, respectful of the ideas of others and appreciative of the glimpse into truth those ideas might offer. No, the point was simply to win the debate. So, the longer the debate lasted, the more my family members would dig in their heels and refuse to budge. In many ways, I watched at Thanksgiving Dinner as my family did its best impression of the approach to Catholic-Protestant dialogue pursued over much of the prior four and a half centuries, both sides digging in their heels and doing their best to distance themselves from the opposite view. After a while, for my family a very brief time, the issue at stake no longer mattered. What mattered was defeating the opposition. For far too long, Roman Catholics were not encouraged, and at times were actively discouraged, from reading the bible because that was what the Protestants did. Once, while offering thoughts on developing a personal relationship with Jesus Christ in a seminary course I was teaching on catechesis in the church, a participant said he could never speak that way in his parish because it was his belief that speaking about a personal relationship with Jesus Christ sounded too Protestant.

No doubt the opposite was also true, with young Protestant Christians being taught to avoid anything that even closely resembled Roman Catholic belief or practice. Some communities went so far as to seemingly deny all truth encountered in the post-canonical period as if God simply ceased speaking to the people so as not to appear too close to the Catholic view of unfolding tradition. Like my family, Protestants and Catholics rejected the views of the other at times simply because they were the views of the other. Giving any credence to the opposition was tantamount to losing the debate, the one outcome that was considered anathema by both sides of the argument. In the Roman Catholic experience, there were calls to engage in intercredal cooperation, the Roman Catholic Church working hand in hand and side by side with Protestant denominations to help rebuild Europe in the aftermath of the Second World War. Those calls were challenged by many in the church who feared that working alongside Protestants might encourage far too many of the faithful to perceive Protestantism as an acceptable form of Christian expression. Christian relativism would set in and that needed to be avoided at all costs, even if that meant we could not work together to help rebuild the world after the devastation of the Second World War.

Although great strides have been made over the past fifty years, some of the bias and stereotype and suspicion remain. A Baptist minister refused to participate in a local ministerium because a Catholic priest belonged to the group. A pastor whose church was right around the corner from a

Conclusion

church where I once ministered offered sermons each Sunday laced with anti-Catholic invective. As a Roman Catholic I have often encountered individual believers who remain highly suspicious of their Protestant brothers and sisters for no reason other than they are members of a Protestant denomination. Protestants are at times disparaged as bible beaters and fanatics, fundamentalists, and traitors. They are often denounced for their alleged belief that the moral life does not matter. As long as you say Jesus is Lord you are saved and free to live however you want, a misunderstanding of the Protestant emphasis on the notion that God alone saves. In my conversations with some of the people who make such claims, it is painfully obvious that they do not understand, nor want to, the beliefs and teachings of other Christian denominations. The need to win the debate is still much too present in my community and, if my conversations with Tom are any indication, the same opposing impulse is all too present among some in the Presbyterian community as well.

The best books both challenge and console. In these pages I hope you have experienced both the challenge of new and different ideas and the consolation of familiar and agreeable ones. In my introduction, I spoke of this book arising from the bonds of friendship. I hope the book has, even in some very small way, strengthened the bonds linking our two faith communities. Or perhaps, more realistically, I hope the book has strengthened the bonds of faith and understanding between neighbors or co-workers who belong to different Christian communities. Creative tension will always exist between two communities who operate from differing interpretations of the same basic narrative. But, growth in knowledge of other traditions can not only breed mutual respect. It can also deepen knowledge of, and commitment to, our own tradition. We can often appreciate the core beliefs and nuances of our faith tradition when we engage in dialogue with the core beliefs and nuances of other faith traditions. Hopefully, for the Roman Catholics and Presbyterians reading this book, you have grown in knowledge of your own tradition and gained a deeper respect for the theological commitments of the other.

Ultimately, I hope the book has made two important contributions. First, it is my hope that, as mentioned above, the book has fostered greater respect and understanding of two rich traditions. Second, and more broadly, I hope the book offers insight into the process of dialogue and disagreement. Regarding the latter contribution, we live in a time in which we have lost or are losing the ability to engage with each other in reasoned, civil discourse and the ability to disagree without demonizing. We live in an age in which, if you disagree with me, you are a bad person and nothing you say has any value. It is disturbing to me that loud voices on college campuses successfully cancel speaking engagements of people with whom they disagree. Rather than promoting the free exchange of ideas and views, too many young people want to drown out anyone who dares disagree with them. Our enemies, in this view, are not so much North Korea, Russia, or Iran. Our enemies are not ISIS or Al Qaeda. Our enemies are the conservative who lives across the hall or the liberal next door.

I earlier referenced the view in our culture that truth is a personal possession. I must speak my truth, live my truth, proclaim my truth. A major problem for this view, and we see it embodied each day in our culture, is that it promotes a conviction in our own infallibility. If I possess my truth, anyone who deigns to disagree with me must be false. That is why our public conversation has become so vitriolic. We have lost the ability to disagree, aided in large part by the limited good that is social media and its ability to create an echo chamber within which our views are championed and any opposing thoughts are mocked and ridiculed. If our country, and we as people, are to survive and thrive, we must be willing to put aside the acrimony that shapes our public and personal conversations and the contributions we make to them. Rather, we must learn again how to speak with each other, to disagree with each other, to recognize that the truth does not belong to me or to you and that we are all involved in a common pursuit of truth. That will not make our disagreements vanish, especially concerning issues about which we passionately disagree, but it will change the way we converse and disagree, allowing us to see each other as friends and not enemies because of the disagreement. Of course, one of the most basic steps we can take in a better and more fruitful direction is a willingness to put down our devices. If we are willing to leave behind the echo chamber and our own self-absorption, we can recover and develop the skills, values, and virtues necessary to renew and refresh our public and interpersonal dialogue. My hope is that this book can stand as an example of two individuals and two communities who disagree but who can disagree with respect, openness, and genuine affection.

Regarding the former contribution, on the surface, readers might draw the conclusion that Roman Catholics and Presbyterians are extremely far apart, representing two drastically different visions of the Christian faith. And to a certain extent, that is true. But, upon closer inspection, it

Conclusion

is my hope that readers also recognize the same basic impulses encountered in their own faith community reflected in the beliefs and theological commitments of the other. Those impulses and commitments lead our two communities down different Christian paths. The Presbyterian path can be generally understood through its emphasis on the absolute sovereignty of God. The path followed by Roman Catholicism can be generally identified with the church's emphasis on the relationship between God and humankind. These differing emphases shape the fundamental beliefs and outlooks of these two Christian traditions and provide a helpful lens through which to see those differences.

These differences, which often represent different emphases rather than different beliefs, can be seen in practically every issue we have raised. Both communities place a great deal of importance on the narrative encountered in the pages of scripture. Presbyterians tend to view the bible as a document out of time, as the product of God, more so than the Roman Catholic contextual view that stresses the interplay between God's inspiration and the human skills and historical context of the various biblical authors and editors. The Catholic belief that the bible did not produce the church but it was the Holy Spirit, inspiring God's people, that produced the bible, creates a fundamentally different understanding of the nature of scripture and its proper interpretation. But, both find within its pages the narratives of the two great ancient communities, Israel and the early followers of Jesus, that stand at the heart of the Christian tradition. To be sure, the difference in approach, understanding, and weight lead at times to significant differences of opinion regarding the appropriate application of biblical teaching in each successive age. And, Presbyterianism seems unwilling to accept the view held by many Catholic scripture scholars that, although we believe the bible to be the inspired word of God, it is a mistake to adopt as infallible every opinion or viewpoint offered by a biblical author. In addition, the Roman Catholic tradition seems more open to theological development within scripture and a greater willingness to distinguish between the time-bound and timeless truths of the biblical tradition. Nevertheless, both communities have a clearly expressed desire to live a life of faithful discipleship shaped by the word of God encountered in both testaments.

Both communities understand that it is God who saves. But, Roman Catholicism emphasizes the relational truth of God's salvation whereas the Presbyterian community understands salvation through the lens of God's absolute sovereignty. The Presbyterian view grows out of a desire to protect and defend the sovereignty of God it saw as under attack or at least insufficiently expressed in the Roman Catholic tradition. This desire to defend God's sovereignty found expression in John Calvin's doctrine of double predestination, that before we even exist God has predestined who will be saved and who will be condemned. The Reformed position proclaims the gracious mercy of God on the grounds that, since humans are all unworthy of salvation, God does not need to save anyone yet chooses to save some. For Presbyterians, such a view emphasizes the sovereignty, justice, and mercy of God. From the perspective of Roman Catholic theology, such a vision suggests, not that God is merciful but that God is capricious, petty, jealous, and judgmental. If God has the power to save all but chooses only to save some, such a decision seems to stand in stark contrast to the God who sent his Son into the world to save it. God, in the Reformed vision, may be a kind dictator, but a dictator remains a dictator. Such a view seems incompatible with God's expressed desire that all be saved.[1]

In reality, Roman Catholicism did not desire to offend or limit God's sovereignty but rather wanted to protect and defend the notion of the goodness of God's creation and the Christian view that salvation is a relational reality. The Roman Catholic theological tradition does not wish to overthrow God's sovereignty. Rather, it seeks to affirm human cooperation with God's sovereignty. God does not force the gift of salvation on us. God created humanity with free will and that the human exercise of free will was rightly and necessarily involved in the process of God's salvation. Emphasizing human cooperation with God in the process of salvation does not undermine the power of God but affirms the loving relationship God hopes will unite us. Despite the different conclusions we draw based upon our location along the spectrum of Christian belief, both communities believe that it is God alone who saves. The traditions, however, approach that truth from opposite ends of the theological spectrum with one declaring a doctrine that proclaims salvation occurs without reference to humankind and the other articulating a belief that salvation involves the expression of a relationship between human beings and the God who saves.

Both traditions celebrate the truth of God's saving love, albeit in different ways and with different understandings. Both find the origin of those celebrations in the life, death, and resurrection of Jesus and the continuing inspiration of the Holy Spirit. These two Christian communities possess very different understandings of the presence and action of the Holy

---

1. 1 Tim. 2: 3-4.

Conclusion

Spirit in the church and obviously possess alternative views flowing from those understandings of the way the church should be structured to accomplish its divine mission. But, neither doubts the presence of the Spirit or the belief that Jesus left behind a community called to action in history in his name on behalf of the kingdom he proclaimed and for which he died and was raised. And both traditions have great respect for those who have come before, passing on to each successive generation the good news of the gospel through their words and deeds. True, because of its theological commitment to the more relational view of Christian faith, the Roman Catholic Church has formalized this respect shaped by its view of the boundary-less church and its beliefs about the importance of the presence of the saints in the church in every age. I summarize these views here not to diminish the differences between our faith communities but to draw attention that, though we may be at different places along the spectrum of Christian belief, we are both on the same spectrum.

One of my favorite professors during my seminary career was a Sulpician priest named Fred Cwiekowski. Fred was not only an outstanding scholar and theologian but a wonderful role model for men preparing to serve the church as ordained priests. The first class I took with Fred was Theological Anthropology, a course that set out to examine what it meant to be human in light of Jesus Christ. I recall during one typically engaging and inspiring lecture, Fred exhorted us to remember that the gospel was and is good news. It was his hope that, during our ministry as priests, we would always remember that the people who originally proclaimed the gospel did so because they believed it was truly good news for all. I left the seminary after five years to marry and soon began the long journey of pursuing my doctorate in theology. And throughout that pursuit, I was often inspired to continue because of Fred's exhortation in my first year as a seminarian. Good news excites us, makes us feel better about life, and gives us hope. It shapes our perspective and can transform our approach to life. Too often, plagued by the struggles of contemporary life, I have forgotten Fred's challenge to his first-year seminarians. But, from my vantage point, I believe my church has at times also forgotten this basic truth. We can get so caught up in the rules and regulations and disturbing moral developments that we can forget that the story of Jesus is, at its core, good news for us all. During the mass, we pray, "Look not on our sins but on the faith of your church . . ." Unfortunately, the church too often focuses on our sins and not nearly enough on our faith. But, looking at both is truly good news for us, reminding us that because of God's love we are more than the sins we commit. We can be better, we can be free, we can become instruments of God's love in our lives and world.

At the end of the day, Presbyterians and Roman Catholics may disagree on numerous issues and may understand the various dimensions of Christian faith in slightly or substantially different ways and those areas of agreement and disagreement are important to consider as we move forward. But, what should always remain true for both traditions in spite of any disagreements we may have is that we are both committed to the proclamation of the good news of Jesus Christ. What we can get hung up on may differ and members of both communities may struggle to better surrender to the good news amidst the daily stresses and strains of contemporary life. Nevertheless, if we are willing to commit ourselves, commit our time, our energy, our passion, our lives to the gospel we too can discover that it is truly good news. Two thousand years later Presbyterians and Roman Catholics can celebrate the simplicity of Mark's gospel alongside the compassionate, justice-seeking, thoughtfulness of Luke and the stunning depth of John. If we had only one of these gospels, our understanding of Jesus would be much less robust and vivid. Thanks to the diversity of the New Testament, we can appreciate the person and significance of Jesus of Nazareth from a variety of perspectives and understandings. Each of those perspectives faithfully, but not uniformly, proclaims the gospel in its own way. So, too, I believe both Presbyterians and Roman Catholics proclaim the good news, albeit from different perspectives and with different understandings of the ramifications of the Christ event. But, rather than seeing those differences as divisive, relationship ending concepts, it is possible to view each community as striving in its own way to faithfully proclaim the gospel and its significance and that through thoughtful, respectful, and loving ongoing dialogue both communities may grow in faith and understanding and deepen our commitment to the good news of the gospel. It is my hope that this book has shed some light on each tradition and the kinds of values we hold and the kinds of questions we continue to ask. But, above all, I hope you the reader walk away with a greater awareness that the story of Jesus of Nazareth and the continuing presence and inspiration of the Holy Spirit are truly good news for us all and feel more powerfully the call to embody that good news each day of your life.

Bibliography

Anselm. *Cur Deus Homo?* Sidney Norton Deane, trans. Fort Worth, TX: RDMc, 2005.
Beveridge, Henry, trans. *John Calvin, Institutes of the Christian Religion.* Peabody, MA: Hendrickson, 2008.
Brown, Raymond E. *A Coming Christ in Advent: Essays on the Gospel Narratives Preparing for the Birth of Jesus (Matthew 1 and Luke 1).* Collegeville, MN: Liturgical Press, 1988.
———. *The Birth of the Messiah: A Commentary on the Infancy Narratives in the Gospels of Matthew and Luke (The Anchor Yale Bible Reference Library).* New York, NY. Doubleday, 1993.
Borg, Marcus J. *Reading the Bible Again for the First Time: Taking the Bible Seriously but Not Literally.* New York, NY: HarperCollins, 2001.
Burghardt, Walter J., S.J. *Still Proclaiming Your Wonders: Homilies for the 80's.* Mahwah, NJ: Paulist Press, 1984.
Calvin, Jean. *Calvin's Commentaries, Volume XVI: Harmony of Matthew, Mark, Luke.* Grand Rapids, MI: Baker Books, 2005.
Carroll, James. *Prince of Peace.* New York, NY: NAL Books, 1985.
Coniaris, Anthony M. *Orthodoxy: A Creed for Today.* Minneapolis, MN: Light and Life Co., 1972.
Cwiekowski, Frederick J. *The Beginnings of the Church.* Mahwah, NJ: Paulist Press, 1988.
Dulles, Avery Cardinal. *Models of the Church.* New York, NY: Doubleday, 2000.
Flannery, Austin, O.P. *Vatican Council II, Volume 1: The Conciliar and Post-Conciliar Documents.* Northport, NY: Costello, 1998.
Geisler, Norman L. *Inerrancy.* Grand Rapids, MI: Zondervan, 1980.
Haight, Roger, S.J. *The Experience and Language of Grace.* Mahwah, NJ: Paulist Press, 1979.
Hodge, Charles. *Systematic Theology.* Grand Rapids, MI: W. B. Eerdmans Company, 1940. Christian Classics Ethereal Library. Web. 8 Feb. 2018. http://www.ccel.org/ccel/hodge/theology1.iii.vi.v_1.html
John Paul II, pope. *Mulieris Dignitatem (On the Dignity and Vocation of Women),* Encyclical Letter of August 15, 1988. Available on the Vatican Web site, http://w2.vatican.va/content/john-paul-ii/en/apost_letters/1988/documents/hf_jp-ii_apl_19880815_mulieris-dignitatem.html
Kelly, Douglas F., Hugh McClure, and Philip B. Rollinson. *The Westminster Confession of Faith: An Authentic Modern Version.* Signal Mountain, TN: Summertown Texts, 1992.
Kelly, J.N.D. *Early Christian Creeds,* 3rd edition. New York: Continuum, 2006.

Bibliography

Kolb, Robert, and Carl R. Trueman. *Between Wittenberg and Geneva: Lutheran and Reformed Theology in conversation*. Grand Rapids, MI: Baker, 2017.

Litfin, Bryan M. *Getting to Know the Church Fathers: An Evangelical Introduction*. Grand Rapids, MI: Brazos Press, 2007.

Marshall, Rosalind K. *John Knox*, Kindle Edition. Edinburgh: Birlinn, 2013.

McBrien, Richard P. *The Church: The Evolution of Catholicism*. New York, NY: HarperCollins, 2008.

McGrath, Alister E. *Christian Theology: An Introduction*, 4th Edition. Malden, MA: Blackwell, 2007.

McPherson, James M. *Drawn with the Sword: Reflections on the American Civil War*. New York, NY: Oxford University Press, 1996.

Olson, Roger E. *The Mosaic of Christian Belief: Twenty Centuries of Unity and Diversity*. Downers Grove, IL: Inter-Varsity Press, 2002.

Pius X, pope. *Vehementer Nos (Our Soul)*. Encyclical Letter of February 11, 1906. Available on the Vatican Web site, http://w2.vatican.va/content/pius-x/en/encyclicals/documents/hf_p-x_enc_11021906_vehementer-nos.html

Shelley, Bruce L. *Church History in Plain Language*. Updated 2nd Edition. Dallas, TX: Word, 1995.

Stark, Rodney. *The Triumph of Christianity: How the Jesus Movement Became the World's Largest Religion*. New York: HarperCollins, 2012.

The Holy See. *Catechism of the Catholic Church*. Washington, D.C.: United States Catholic Conference, 1994.

Wright, N.T. *Surprised by Hope: Rethinking Heaven, the Resurrection, and the Mission of the Church*. New York, NY: HarperCollins, 2008.

www.ingramcontent.com/pod-product-compliance
Lightning Source LLC
Chambersburg PA
CBHW070742160426
43192CB00009B/1539